Principal Talk!

The Art of Effective Communication in Successful School Leadership

Cheli Cerra, M.Ed. & Ruth Jacoby, Ed.D.

JOSSEY-BASS
A Wiley Imprint
www.josseybass.com

ISBN: 0-7879-7911-2

Printed in the United States of America
FIRST EDITION

10 9 8 7 6 5 4 3 2 1

The Buzz About *Principal Talk!*

"Principals are constantly communicating with parents, teachers, community leaders, and school board members. Effective communication is the key to their success as administrators. The authors of Principal Talk! *have provided useful tips and effective strategies to assist every administrator to become the professional communicator expected of them. This book belongs in every principal's office!"*

Gary Babin, Assistant Superintendent
LaFourche Parish Schools
Thibodaux, Louisiana

"Principal Talk! *is an excellent guide for the effective school principal and recognized community leader. The authors, Cerra and Jacoby, have made a valuable analysis of numerous situations involving a principal's relationships with teachers, students, parents, supervisors, superintendents, school board members, and other community leaders. Principal Talk! provides refreshing insight and criteria for self-evaluation into one's own pattern of communication."*

Irving Flinker, Ret.
Former principal of the
Gershwin Jr. H.S. Brooklyn, New York

"Cerra and Jacoby have done their homework. Principal Talk! *is a must-have manual for any aspiring or even veteran principal. The communication techniques, advice, and easy-to-read format will make you a winner in successful school leadership."*

Eric "Jerry" Parker
38-year career educator/administrator

This book is dedicated
to our dads: Antonio "Nico"
and Theodore "Teddy."
Thanks for being great fathers and
instilling in us the values that made
us the leaders we are today.

The Art of Effective Communication

As I live my life, I understand what it means to communicate.

* ✳ I begin to open myself to change and new ideas.

* ✳ I begin to evaluate my own progress.

* ✳ I begin to allow others to provide constructive criticism.

* ✳ I begin to communicate effectively with everyone.

* ✳ I begin to attend workshops for personal and professional growth.

* ✳ I begin to listen to others.

* ✳ I begin to share ideas and knowledge with others.

* ✳ I begin to be persuasive.

* ✳ I begin to be objective.

* ✳ I begin to be well prepared.

* ✳ I begin to be effective.

* ✳ I begin to be reflective.

I have P.O.W.E.R.!

www.school-talk.com

Table of Contents

How to Use This Book

The snapshots you find throughout this book reflect real-life situations a principal faces in dealing with students, teachers, parents, school and district staff, the school board, and community. The book is divided into five chapters. Common situations, as well as those that are not so common, are presented, followed by strategies, communication tips, and worksheets to support each point.

By utilizing these tools you will become:

- Proactive.
- Organized.
- A Good Record-Keeper.
- An Accurate Reporter of Information.

But most of all you will be a successful school leader. Use the "Points to Ponder" to delve deeper into each scenario's agenda and learn how to develop a guide to creating a smooth course of action. By using the checklists, worksheets, and letters, you will become skillful and confident in communicating important points to students, teachers, parents, staff, the school board, and the community. You will present yourself as the consummate professional during a face-to-face meeting, in a phone conference, or by Internet contact. By using the worksheets and preparing in advance whenever possible, you will find you have extra time to research additional resources you may want to recommend, such as websites, school personnel, outside agencies, books, magazines, and district personnel. As the educational leader of the school, you will be the one others look to for guidance.

www.School-talk.com

How to Use This Book

Read the snapshots and tips to gain insight to a problem similar to the one you might be facing or about to encounter. Your real-life situations may include elements of multiple snapshots. You can mix and match and adapt them to fit your comfort zone and individual circumstance. Use the tip information and the worksheets as needed to guide you through each situation. These keys, tips, and worksheets will assist you in communicating successfully.

Before you turn the page, we recommend that as your first step in your journey toward becoming an effective communicator you take the **Communication Skills Assessment** *on page 13*. This will help you determine your level of comfort when communicating with all school stakeholders. Recognize both your areas of strengths and those areas that need some additional assistance and development.

Our goal in writing this book is to give you insight, information, and practice tips you can use to establish a positive working relationship with everyone who crosses your path and assists you in continuing to be or to become a high-performing school site leader.

Points To Ponder:

Use the *"Points to Ponder"* at the end of each chapter to delve deeper into each scenario's agenda and learn how to develop a guide to creating a smooth course of action.

Communication Skills Assessment Pre-Test/Post-Test

Directions: Check "Y" for Yes and "N" for No to give the response you find most appropriate.

☐Y ☐N   1.   I am comfortable speaking with parents, school board members, and teachers.

☐Y ☐N   2.   I listen more than I talk.

☐Y ☐N   3.   I value parent, teacher, and staff input.

☐Y ☐N   4.   I encourage parents to visit my school.

☐Y ☐N   5.   I anticipate and welcome questions.

☐Y ☐N   6.   I come prepared to meetings.

☐Y ☐N   7.   I research solutions and methods when I do not know the answers.

☐Y ☐N   8.   I like to invite parents, school board members, and members of the press to the school.

☐Y ☐N   9.   I do not believe that I know more than the teachers and staff.

☐Y ☐N   10.   I do not mind if a member of the press calls for my opinion.

☐Y ☐N   11.   I make eye contact at all meetings.

☐Y ☐N   12.   I respect the opinion of parents, school board members, and the press.

☐Y ☐N   13.   I don't feel uncomfortable when having to deal with an upset parent.

☐Y ☐N   14.   I smile and greet parents, students, and teachers each morning and afternoon.

☐Y ☐N   15.   I initiate parent and staff contact immediately as concerns arise.

☐Y ☐N   16.   I am at ease when talking with staff and parents about difficult situations.

☐Y ☐N   17.   I communicate frequently with parents and staff.

☐Y ☐N   18.   I admit to staff and parents when I do not know an answer and get back to them when I find out information they need.

☐Y ☐N   19.   I have an "Open Door Policy" where parents and staff know that they can see me when concerns arise.

☐Y ☐N   20.   I am at ease when speaking in front of large groups.

If you scored 18 or higher, you are on your way to becoming an effective communicator.

If you scored 15 to 18, you may want to read carefully those snapshots addressing areas in which you are weak and practice the authors' techniques. The other snapshots may give you further insight and communication skills to benefit your own conversational style.

If you scored below 15, you will want to read all the chapters and snapshots. Practice the techniques, asking your friends and family to assist you. When you are ready to use the techniques, you may want to start by applying them in more simple situations or by talking with those whom you feel comfortable before you tackle the more difficult scenarios.

oduction

"My only advice is to stay aware, listen carefully, and yell for help if you need it."
Judy Blume

Introduction

Congratulations! By reading this book you are taking the first step toward acquiring those essential skills that will serve you for a lifetime as an effective communicator.

Let's face it—everyone needs to communicate. But effective communication is more than just talking—it encompasses pursuing a deeper understanding, an open sharing of ideas, the willingness to brainstorm without criticizing, and the effective dissemination of information. It means getting to the core of what we are all about. Tact and skill in handling people are enviable traits in any profession, but for the successful school leader, they are essential. *Principal Talk!* will show you how you can acquire or enhance these skills and then utilize them effectively.

Imagine taking a snapshot of a situation and being able to assess it. In the following pages, you will find fifty-two snapshots we have captured for you. These snapshots portray a variety of situations principals may encounter. Accompanying each snapshot will be strategies you can immediately put to use to direct the outcome of each situation to the benefit of everyone involved. As you practice these skills and become a better communicator, you will not only acquire a tremendous feeling of personal power, but you will also find students, teachers, parents, staff, school board members, and the community leaders responding positively to your confidence and ability. By building on this bridge of effective communication, you will be able to head off many potential problems before they arise and be the successful leader you need to be.

Successful school principals understand the needs of their students, teachers, parents, staff, school board members, and the community. As a leader, you have to be strong. You have to be willing to walk in front of your faculty and staff and tackle a problem. Remember, you reap what you sow. If you allow the people who work on your team to be less than the best, if you do not set high expectations and high levels of professionalism, you will end up with less than positive results. Learn to be humble, but not shy or timid. Be proud. Take pride in your accomplishments; celebrate success. Embrace humor. Learn to laugh. Accept life as it is. Being a leader in today's society is quite different than in the past. Leadership has evolved into a more shared, collective, cooperative, democratic process. Yes, the buck has to stop with you. But a successful principal knows how to work with her faculty and staff—not have them work for her. She knows how to empower; she knows how to bring out leadership in all of her team members, even those who have always been followers.

Introduction

A succesful principal creates a work environment where professionals are in continued growth and development. Learn to develop your skills as a leader. Find your own style. What might work well for your colleague may not work well for you. Do your due diligence. Know which battles to pick and which to let go. Know when to get tough and when to be soft. Know your teachers, your staff, your community, your parents, the strengths and weaknesses of the school, and the needs of your students. Above all know yourself.

Knowing how to communicate well is the mark of the true leader and can transform a competent principal into a great one. When you follow the techniques offered in the following pages, you will be on your way to succeeding in achieving this goal.

Communication is the genuine exchange of information, ideas, and thoughts, whereby an agreement is reached, a schedule is established, a goal is promoted, or a conflict is resolved. By using the techniques in this book, this exchange can become a positive learning and teaching experience.

Introduction

As an effective communicator, I will be . . .

Proactive and Professional

As a principal and leader, I will speak out as an advocate for my school, faculty and staff, parents, and students. I will work to convince the public and the media that schools are doing terrific things with student and parent education and that we will continue to provide the best quality education possible by ensuring the safe environment and high academic standards needed to prepare all students for the future.

Organized

I will keep my appointment calendar up-to-date and balance my time so I am available for teachers, staff, parents, and students as well as district personnel, community, and school board members.

Well Prepared

I realize that it is important to keep current on issues and facts to present myself as a professional at all meetings. I will join educational organizations to keep up with current educational research and trends. I promise to read all emails and respond in an appropriate amount of time. Before entering a dialogue with the faculty, staff, or parents, I will be informed of the situation and issues. I will use data analysis to understand the test scores from one marking period to another and from one year to another. I will also use other appropriate information to evaluate progress. I will apply the information gained to make any necessary changes, and to make improvements in programs and instruction for the coming school year.

Communication is an exchange of information. If you are not engaging in an exchange, you are not communicating.

Notes: _____

_____

_____

_____

_____

_____

_____

_____

_____

_____

Chapter One

Leadership Success

> "I don't know everything, I just do everything."
> **Toni Morrison**

Overview

Let's face it. Principals do everything! You are an educational leader, hall monitor, nurse, counselor, custodian, traffic cop, negotiator, mediator, arbitrator, accountant, coach, disciplinarian, keeper of the peace, advocate, marketer, public relations specialist—the list goes on and on. I don't know about you, but the reason we chose to be principals—besides wanting to make a difference in the lives of children—is that there is definitely never a dull moment. Your day-to-day tasks are as unpredictable as they are predictable. Yes, you have your procedures and routines, but you also have hair-pulling moments that keep your blood pumping. Multi-tasking is definitely part of the job requirement.

What makes a great and successful school leader? As successful leaders we have written this book to share our experiences, give you practical information, and assist you in honing your skills. This book is not research-based but experienced-based, drawing upon the situations, strategies, advice, and activities we have followed in our schools. The end result has been success—and we want you to be successful too.

Successful school principals:

- Have and share a vision;
- Communicate effectively with all school stakeholders;
- Keep everyone safe;
- Promote a positive school climate;
- Understand the needs of children, parents, teachers, staff, and their own; and
- Lead with love.

The Snapshots:

1. A Vision to Be Shared
2. Safety First
3. To Market, to Market
4. Be Visible

Snapshot #1:
A Vision to Be Shared

Vice Principal Perfect has just been promoted to Principal of Middletown Middle School. As he begins his assignment he notices that the goals and vision that he has in mind are not shared by everyone. How should he handle this?

Tip: How often do principals end one year or start the next with a goal in mind to create a school's vision and mission or, in simpler terms, to have a "purpose." Many times it is a year-long process involving meeting after meeting with teachers, community leaders, parents, and administrators. Sometimes the report written on all this is pages long. Does anyone remember it? Is everyone committed to it? Better yet, does everyone on the faculty and staff know it, especially new teachers? A well-written vision statement shows you how to measure each step of the way, so you know whether you have reached the achievement goals. The mission statement flows directly from the vision statement. It outlines the course you must follow and what actions you must take to achieve the vision. The mission is a continuous process and must be assessed periodically so necessary adjustments can occur. A vision and a mission should be created, shaped, and formed by all school stakeholders.

> **The vision statement is the BIG picture.**

> **The mission statement is more of a "how to" guide.**

Snapshot #2:
Safety First

www.school-talk.com

Keep safety first..

A t dismissal Veronica's mother approaches you and asks you if you have seen her child. You help her locate the classroom teacher and begin to try to find Veronica. You make an "all call" over the PA system but Veronica is still not found. Veronica's mother begins to get hysterical—she cannot find her daughter. You bring Veronica's mother into the office and begin to calm the mother down and ask her to make several phone calls to see if she has gone home with a friend. After a while you find out that Veronica took the school bus home. In the future, what should you do?

Tip : The safety and security of all staff and students is your responsibility. Start off right by knowing how your students go home. Communicate in writing the arrival and dismissal procedures to parents, teachers, and staff on the first day of school. Have a rainy day procedure as well as an emergency procedure—make sure that everyone knows what to do and where to go. When it comes to school bus transportation, make sure that bus drivers provide rides only to students eligible to ride the bus. Also communicate to parents that bus students will only be allowed to get on and off at their designated bus stop. In case of a bus delay, have emergency numbers on hand to contact parents. It's important for students and parents to know the policies and procedures. It is wise to know in writing how the students go home to alleviate any unnecessary confusion. You can use the **School Year Dismissal Information Worksheet** *on page 25* to collect this information for your school files. In this case, either the student or the parent got confused as to what the transportation plan was for this day.

School Year Dismissal Information Worksheet

Dear Parent (s),

To provide for the safe dismissal of all students, we must be informed regarding the individual arrangements for each student.

Please provide the information requested below and return immediately to your child's teacher. Your cooperation is appreciated and will provide us with the necessary information for your child's safe arrival home daily.

Child's Name _____ **Grade** _____ **Room Number** _____
Teacher's Name _____
Home Telephone Number _____ **Mobile** _____
Beeper Number _____ **Email** _____

Please complete/check-off appropriate areas:

☐ **Parent Pick-Up**
☐ **Public School Bus Route #** _____
☐ **Private Bus—Name** _____ **Phone** _____
☐ **After Care** _____
☐ **Walks Home** (must sign permission letter and have on file at school)

Sincerely,

Principal

Permission Letter

Dear Parents,

You have indicated on the Dismissal Information form that you give permission for your child _____ to walk home from school.

Please sign below if this is correct and remember to advise your child's teacher whenever dismissal arrangements change.

Thank you,

Principal

Parent Signature_____ **Date**_____

Student Name _____ **Date** _____

Snapshot #3:

To Market, to Market

With school choice comes competition and the jobs of faculty and staff may depend on positive school marketing.

Your enrollment is down by 200 students and you are in jeopardy of losing several teachers and critical support staff. There are three weeks left before the first day of school. You have done your homework and found that a charter school has just opened several blocks away. How should you handle this?

Tip : For decades, principals have had the same job description, which basically said, "run the school." All they had to do was hire and fire staff, keep parents happy, schedule classes, run meetings, and make sure students were learning—in other words, do everything possible to keep things running smoothly. They had accountability, but nothing like the demands of this century. Not only do principals have to maintain smooth operations, they also have to market their school, fund raise, and garner support for new programs.

Think of the commercials and ads of the most popular products. Do they change frequently? Not those that are successful. Are they easy to replicate? Find something that sets your school "above the crowd" and give it a theme, a catch phrase, a jingle. Then repeat, repeat, and repeat it some more. Say it so often that everyone in the school and outside the school environment remembers it. If it is heard often enough and seen in all your handouts, the public will (start to believe it. Isn't this what McDonald's and Wendy's do? Isn't that what Burger King means when they insist, "Have it your way.")

Education is foremost on the minds of politicians and voters. Everyone has an opinion on how to improve education and how to spend taxpayers' money on educational issues and schools in general. Principals are becoming the main marketers for their schools. However, this is not the job of one person. The entire school and its stakeholders need to assist. Every time a person says something about your school, someone else is listening. Get the word out on the positive impressions. It is imperative to celebrate the "successes" of the school, whether it's about teachers, students, parents, programs, the PTA, or anything else that shows what a good job your school is doing.

Snapshot #4:
Be Visible

You are inundated with paperwork and have begun to stay more and more in your office and less and less in the hallways. You begin to realize that this has had a negative impact on students and there are more behavior problems than ever before. How should you handle this?

Tip : First learn to effectively delegate. The proper delegation of work is not "passing the buck" but rather an effective method to promote the professional growth and development of others. When you assign this work you should have a conversation as to why you have selected this staff member to complete this task. Utilize all of the resources that you have at hand to assist you in dealing with the "paper tiger." Every year it seems that there is more and more paper work, but coming up with an efficient system will make the difference between a smooth-running school and one that is running ineffectively. Remember, you have to be visible! One of the best ways to find a system is to network and talk to other principals. You will be surprised how the students' behaviors seem to improve once the principal is out and in full view. Creating a positive school environment that is safe and productive should become a priority for everyone.

www.school-talk.com

Manage your time to allow maximum contact with students, faculty, and staff.

Points To Ponder:

PONDER

How do you create "buy in"?

POINTS

- Post the vision and mission statement in the main office and in each classroom.
- Make sure every newsletter and handout has the vision statement in bold print on the top of the page.
- Include the vision statement in every advertisement and morning broadcast.
- Focus on the present and the future goals.
- Build positive and beneficial teams that assist in keeping the vision, mission, and goals in the forefront of all agendas.

PONDER

More than likely, most principals were neither marketing nor business majors. More likely their fields were education and leadership. Yet principals are asked to wear so many more hats these days. How does one go about becoming a master marketer?

POINTS

- Whenever there is a meeting, talk up the "school's happenings."
- Survey parents, teachers, and students. Analyze the information gathered and decide on the items that need to be changed. Do this with a team of stakeholders.
- Design a brochure that illustrates the uniqueness and positive qualities of your school. Put quotes in it from students and parents who articulate why they like your school and what qualities make it shine. Pass this out to new parents, media, and community businesses like real estate offices and local newspapers.
- Promote positive PR. Be visible at all school events from student performances to parent meetings. This pays off in the long run ten times over.

Chapter Two

The School Team

> "Give a little to a child and you get a great deal back."
> **John Ruskin**

Overview

Unlike a competition, where individuals are pitted against each other, educators are moving toward the team approach for planning and sharing ideas. This concept eliminates the need to be competitive and allows all staff to focus on the most important objectives—setting and meeting high expectations for each student.

This chapter deals with bringing teachers and school personnel together who will meet standards set forth by the nation, state, and district, by the school's mission, and by each other to achieve the common goal of student success. Principals will recognize and find ideas on how to bring all the stakeholders together so they will become partners in the process.

www.school-talk.com

The Snapshots :

5. The School Secretary Is Rude
6. Too Many Referrals
7. Teachers Talking in the Wrong Place
8. An Experienced Teacher Can't Take It Anymore
9. Cafeteria Rudeness
10. Assessing and Testing Too Much
11. If I Teach Physical Education, Why Do I Need to Know About Reading Skills?
12. A Paraprofessional Uses Inappropriate Comments
13. One Week Into the Job a New Teacher Announces, "I Quit"
14. Teacher Knows Her Lessons But Cannot Execute Them
15. The School Brochure Is Not Quite to Your Liking
16. Teacher Switches Grade Level and Starts to Lack Confidence

Snapshot #5:
The School Secretary Is Rude

You receive a call from an irate parent: "Every time I call to ask a question, the secretary is not just unhelpful, she is impolite." This is not the first complaint you've received. Numerous other parents have come into your office on different occasions to complain about the same school secretary being rude, disrespectful, and "short" with them when they call or ask questions. She didn't exhibit those traits when you hired her. You respect her and the job she does. How should you handle this?

Tip : Call the secretary in your office and close the door. Let her know of the complaints and listen to what she has to say. It may be that she is trying to do more than her share and this creates stress for her. Have a copy of her job description handy for you two to discuss. Depending on your relationship with her, you may want to ask what's wrong and if you can help her to make an effort to change her demeanor. You may need to observe the activity and workload at the front desk during prime times. She might simply be overwhelmed and you may be able to change some of her responsibilities or get her assistance during the peak hours of the day. Ask if she may have some suggestions on how to make the office run more efficiently. Explain to her the importance of her job; how she is the first person people see at the school each day. Because of her position, she gives the first impression of the school to all who come through the door. Listen and then offer your suggestions. A compromise or a resolution should be reached, with both of you agreeing that the school's greeter must always be welcoming and helpful and wear a smile.

> *Remember, first impressions can be lasting ones.*

Snapshot #6:
Too Many Referrals

An art teacher sends an average of ten referrals to your office daily. This not only keeps you from attending to your other daily duties, it annoys the other teachers as well. Parents and teachers alike complain that she has no control in her classroom. How should you handle this?

Tip : This teacher needs immediate assistance. Act as a mentor by coming up with an exact classroom design for her and offer other staff to assist. Team her up with one of your top teachers, perhaps one at her grade level or a department chairperson, and have her observe the classroom in action. Ask this teacher to work with her and assist in coming up with a classroom discipline plan. Meet with her on a regular basis to see whether she has made appropriate changes. Remember, even if the referrals stop, the classroom management may not have changed, so continue to monitor the situation.

Other actions you can take are to offer suggestions and other resources; provide a timeline for improvement; and suggest or require that she attend workshops on classroom management, which might be available online.

You may want to work with the district on this plan. Make sure you date and sign all conferences with her, documenting them as official write-ups. Have another administrator present at all meetings.

> *Mentors illuminate knowledge and understanding.*

Snapshot #7:

Teachers Talking in the Wrong Place

Two teachers coming out of a team meeting begin arguing loudly in the main lobby. One says he thinks the changes the principal is making are all wrong and will only create unnecessary paperwork. The other disagrees, saying the new system will make teachers more accountable. The quarrel turns nasty as they insult each other with such accusations as "incompetent" and "stupid and lazy." Parents, colleagues, and students hear these comments. How should you handle this?

Tip: Meet with each teacher separately to gain background information. Decide how you want to proceed and then call them in together. You can choose to let them blow off steam and hope the problem passes or confront them directly. Tell them they both acted unprofessionally. In the future, you'd like them to discuss their disagreements in a private place and in a professional manner. If the teacher doesn't like a new policy, ask him to come to you so he can find out firsthand why a change is being considered. Give them a warning that, if it happens again, there will be an official conference for the record. Teachers have a right to disagree with policy changes but should be encouraged to see you, the principal, when further explanation is needed.

All members of the faculty and staff should be civil and professional with one another.

Snapshot #8:

An Experienced Teacher Can't Take It Anymore

A teacher comes to you, extremely distressed, asking to speak with you privately. Once you close your office door, she breaks down, sobbing that her personal life is a mess and she just can't face the students anymore. She gives you her immediate notice; she won't be back after today. How should you handle this?

Tip : Is the teacher just having a bad day? Listen to her and try to provide assistance. Are there any school board programs or resources that can assist her in her crisis? If so, recommend them. Let her know that you are there to help and assist her. You may want to recommend that she stay home for a day or two and rest. However, if her decision is final do not try to dissuade her. Respect her decision. Be sympathetic. Then quickly look to fill her position. Bring in your staff and assistants and brainstorm on all the people you know who could possibly take over—perhaps one of your substitutes or maybe a friend or relative of one of the staff who may have an interest and have the credentials to be an interim teacher. If these avenues prove unsuccessful, call the district and work with the human resources or personnel department.

Listen first and then find a solution.

As soon as you can, advise the parents of your plan and assure them you will get the best possible teacher for their child's class. Inform them that your grade-level department chairperson and/or team leader is sharing her lessons with the replacement and their child's education will not be disrupted but will continue to be of top quality. When you find the perfect successor, let the parents know by letter, including a summary of the new teacher's background and why you personally think she is the perfect match for the school and their child. You may want to invite parents in for an open house to meet and greet the new instructor.

Snapshot #9: Cafeteria Rudeness

A kindergarten child went home and told his mother that the lady in the cafeteria with the red hair yelled at him because he forgot his lunch money. She raised her voice so all his friends knew that he didn't have any money in his account. She also said he was lucky she gave him lunch at all, but she won't do it again until he brings some money in. The mom calls you that same afternoon yelling at you to do something about this staff member. How should you handle this?

Tip : Call the cafeteria worker into your office. Give her a chance to tell her side of the story. Make it clear that at your school you promote positive attitudes toward children. As the adult, she should know the proper way to speak to children, and that yelling is unacceptable. Remind her of the money collection regulations and that the responsibility does not fall on the child, but on the parent or guardian. A note should go home with the child and the teacher should be informed so he can remind the child or even call the parent. Give the cafeteria worker a warning. Let her know if it happens again, there will be a conference for the record.

When a complaint about a staff member is made, speak to the employee immediately.

Snapshot #10: Assessing and Testing Too Much

Ms. Quiz seems to prefer testing rather than teaching her students. When you visit her room, all you see is "drill to kill." The poor third graders look tense and frustrated, and parents are complaining. How should you handle this?

Tip: Meet with the teacher and review your goals and the school's mission, which should state that all children need to learn. You need to explain to her the importance of analyzing her data and that to test, test, and test is not good teaching. Testing does not legitimize that a teacher has taught a skill; she must know each and every student in her room has gained that skill. Share the **Standardized Testing Percentiles Worksheet** *on page 39* with her. Classes have a variety of students coming from many cultures, with multiple learning styles, and functioning at various skill levels. One lesson-oriented test does not fulfill the needs of every pupil. Creating a portfolio with an acknowledgement of skills gained and skills that need re-teaching is the way to best serve the student population.

Every child learns at his own pace.

Standardized Testing Percentiles Worksheet

TEACHER: GRADE(S):   SCHOOL YEAR:

Student Name (Last, First)	ESE	LEP	IEP	Reading %	Math %	Writing %	Last Year's % (s)	+/- Gain/Loss

1. Have the teachers fill in last year's percentages at the beginning of the school year.
   Note: Highlight in yellow any child who was below grade level the past year. Write in the ESL/LEP level or, if the child has an IEP, note exceptionality-related services in the appropriate column.

2. At the end of the school year, have staff finish the columns by filling in the new percentages. The last column is of prominent importance. You and the teacher can analyze the year-to-year gain or loss for each student and review the overall performance of the class as a whole.

Snapshot #11:

If I Teach Physical Education, Why Do I Need to Know About Reading Skills?

" **I** teach physical education. That is what I am trained to do and what you hired me for. The contract never said anything about reading. What is this about teaching reading skills?" The PE teacher brings this up at a faculty meeting after listening and attending a workshop about the importance of reading across the curriculum. His students are failing his subject because they can't read the health textbook, yet he still doesn't grasp that good reading skills are important. How can he expect them to understand the content if they are not reading on grade level? How should you handle this?

www.schoolTalk.com

Tip : You don't want to answer this teacher by criticizing him in front of the entire faculty. Maybe there are others who feel the same way. Take a deep breath, reflect, and then prepare your answer which should be a summary of what the workshop lecturer just spoke about. Make the point that critical content is important and that all the teacher's students need to understand the content. Remind him that teaching is about reaching all students every single day. Every subject, even physical education, includes some reading. It's his job to know how to help the poor readers as well as the good ones.

Sometimes you may need to remind your staff why they went into teaching.

Snapshot #12:

A Paraprofessional Uses Inappropriate Comments

A paraprofessional is caught by several parents making inappropriate comments to a student at dismissal time. One of the parents who overheard her words comes to you and complains, demanding that something be done immediately. You are already running late for a faculty meeting. How should you handle this?

Tip : Thank her for bringing the issue to your attention and assure her you will address the situation as soon as you can. After the staff meeting or first thing the next morning, call the paraprofessional into your office. Present the complaint made and listen to what the paraprofessional has to say. You may want another administrator present. Depending on the nature of the comment she made to the student, you may need to take further action. Review your code of conduct for employees from your staff handbook. Give advice and remind the paraprofessional of her duties and responsibilities and the policies and procedures of the job.

> **Repeat information to summarize what was said and that it was understood by all the parties.**

Snapshot #13:

One Week Into the Job a New Teacher Announces, "I Quit"

You've had a tough day. You have dealing with an angry parent over class placement, a child temporarily reported as lost, and another child receiving a minor bruise in aftercare. You're just about to go home and relax when one of the new teachers marches into your office and announces, "I quit." After teaching for just one week, she feels overwhelmed and can see she's not cut out to be a teacher. She's already decided to take a position in her father's real estate firm. How should you handle this?

Tip: First, take many deep breaths, which will calm you and give you time to think of a very good response. Tell her to sit down and explain further how she feels and what exactly she is finding the most difficult. Be a good listener! Take notes if you have to so you can repeat back exactly what she told you. Even though she truly might be overwhelmed, show kindness and offer to mentor her. Let her know you feel she has the makings of a good teacher, and that is why you hired her. Ask her to give it a try and reiterate that you and your faculty members are there to assist her whenever she needs you. Everyone is "at risk" at some point during one's lifetime. Suggest that she postpone her decision until a time when she is less stressed and can unemotionally consider all options.

Have an open-door policy for all staff.

Provide a positive acknowledgement for each staff member at least once a year.

Snapshot #14:
Teacher Knows Her Lessons But Cannot Execute Them

Often when you go into Ms. Smart's classroom to observe, you notice she is not following the lesson plans you reviewed. Though her lessons are great on paper, her teaching methods are not. You are afraid that her students will not complete the grade-level skills needed to successfully move on to the next grade. How should you handle this?

Tip: Have a conference with her and explain your expectations for your teachers and students. Ask how she feels she is doing and go from there. It might be beneficial to use an evaluation form that allows you and her to evaluate her performance and compare the results. You may want to use the **Informal Teacher Assessment Worksheet** *on page 46* to assist you. This will give you a basis for dialogue as you review the form line-by-line and discuss it. Let her explain her point of view and then you can share yours.

Other good ideas are: get a colleague or team member to mentor her; send her to workshops; offer her books to read and websites to review; place a substitute in her room so she is free to observe some of the more effective teachers on your staff; and send some exemplary teachers into her room to observe and have them conference with her afterwards to give her their suggestions.

Good teaching is both an art and a science.

Effective teachers create student success!

43

Snapshot #15:
The School Brochure Is Not Quite to Your Liking

Your assistant principal, Miss Write, worked all day on the new school brochure. Unfortunately, you are not happy with the results. You find the layout difficult to follow and the text too wordy. You know Miss Write worked extremely hard and is quite proud of her accomplishment. She is eager to please and easily upset. How should you handle this?

Tip: Call your assistant principal in and thank her for all of her hard work. You can then add that you know how hard she worked on the brochure and you appreciate her efforts. Now comes that "But . . ." Gently give her your first impressions, perhaps referring to it as a great first draft. You could mention that your instructions weren't clear or now that you see it, you have some additional ideas to incorporate. Assistant principals are very busy people. You may suggest that instead of her doing the work herself, she work with a committee of several talented staff members who are artistic and techie savvy. She can oversee and delegate the work and use the committee to review the draft and make constructive suggestions. Offer to set aside part of the next day to work with her. Your mission is to produce the brochure just the way you want it, while not hurting her feelings.

> **Remember to be sensitive to your staff's feelings.**

Snapshot #16:
Teacher Switches Grade Level and Starts to Lack Confidence

Last June, a veteran teacher set her mind on making a change. You both decided at your exit meeting that she could give kindergarten a chance. Yet when school starts, you observe she is struggling with her new class. She especially has difficulty adjusting to the widely divergent skills of kindergarteners. You can see her losing her enthusiasm and you both realize that a terrible mistake has been made. How should you handle this?

Tip: Meet with her and offer suggestions based on what you have seen in the other kindergarten rooms. Assure her that you know she is an excellent teacher and that you don't want her to lose heart. Team her up with one of your best kindergarten teachers and let her visit her room to observe and to gain insights on how to work with younger students.

It might be beneficial for her to attend professional workshops that focus on the primary grades. There she can learn classroom management techniques and curriculum and have a chance to discuss ideas with others who may be having similar problems. Make time to work with her. Observe and provide feedback. As the educational leader, it is important to visit the grade-level, department, and/or team meeting to see what the concerns are. Have the teachers provide you with minutes of the meeting. Use the **Grade-level/Team Meetings Minutes Form** *on page 131* in Appendix A to assist you. Doing this will help you become familiar with the teachers who are showing signs of struggling.

Remember to ask: "How are you today? How are things going in your classroom? Can I assist you with anything?"

Make sure each teacher understands the curriculum and the skills to be taught.

Informal Teacher Assessment Worksheet

Directions: Have the teacher do the assessment first. Then, the evaluator—either you or your designee—completes the second column using the same criteria. Finally, compare the responses in the two columns to open up a dialogue on areas of strengths and weaknesses.

Put the appropriate score in the box:
1 - Not observed
2 - Needs Assistance (Would benefit from a mentor and attending professional workshops)
3 - Performing (Shows evidence of the criteria most of the time)
4 - Exemplary (Consistently shows evidence and would be a great mentor or team leader for others)

Date: _____ Teacher's Name: _____ Grade: _____

Evaluator's Name and Position: _____

Criteria	Staff	Evaluator
Has adequate plan book		
Has state benchmarks for each lesson		
Prompt, efficient, and consistent in grading		
Lesson plans touch on all learning modalities		
Keeps student assessment and portfolios up-to-date		
Demonstrates professional growth		
Keeps emergency lesson plans for substitutes on hand		
Interacts positively with parents (orally and in writing)		
Is punctual and has good attendance		
Dresses professionally		
Anticipates, addresses, and follows through on behavioral concerns		
Uses a variety of teaching strategies		
Mixes small and large group instructions		
Demonstrates good classroom management		
Attends all grade-level, department, and/or team and faculty meetings		
Meets deadlines for all paperwork to administration (report cards, lessons, charts, notes)		
Demonstrates knowledge on all subject matter		
Uses positive words and praise to build student self-esteem		

Criteria	Staff	Evaluator
Gives parents and students clear, specific, and timely feedback		
Familiar with the teacher handbook		
Follows through on administration and/or parent requests		
Enforces limits with conflict resolution		
Is tolerant of students with differences and treats students equally		
Accepts criticism		
Ensures that students are well-supervised at all times		
Handles classroom incidents and emergencies effectively		
Dedicates part of class lessons to review and practice; clear examples are demonstrated		
Keeps classroom attractive and safe and rotates student's work		
Adheres to policies, practices, and procedures stated on job description and in staff handbook		
Sets high expectations for students		
Uses data to construct appropriate lessons and assessments		
Notifies administration of absences in a timely manner		
Maintains a curriculum that provides a variety of activities and materials		
Implements rules on behavior firmly and consistently		

Teacher's Signature: _____ Date: _____ Evaluator's Signature: _____ Date: _____

Evaluator's Comments: _____

_____

Teacher's Comments: _____

_____

Points To Ponder:

PONDER

What makes a high quality school? Can we still operate schools with the same old theories and practices?

POINTS

To be more productive, to keep staff more involved, to produce higher achieving students, and to increase community and parental awareness, try some of the following:

- Disperse tasks to small teams. Teams can reflect, problem solve, plan activities, and coach one another.
- Set clear goals for accountability and assessment.
- Share long-range goals with the entire staff and constantly update.
- Share the vision with all school stakeholders from students to teachers to janitors to parents and community leaders.
- Concentrate on job satisfaction for employees.
- Allow employees to be part of the decision-making process, the setting of long-range goals, and analyzing the vision.
- Know failures are going to occur, but offer encouragement to change and to move forward.
- Become a clear communicator.
- Listen to the community needs and decisions.
- Speak clearly when communicating with the community.
- Remind staff that they are an essential part of the customer service department for your school.

PONDER

Are you worried that new teachers are not working to their fullest potential? Are they getting the help they need to do their very best? Is there a plan in place so they don't get off to a bad start?

POINTS

Work with new staff:

- Find out if the district has an induction program in place.
- Plan and design a mentorship program with all your grade-level, department chairpersons, and/or team leaders and assistant principal. Designate who will assist in carrying out the program throughout the year and who will work with whom.
- Make sure there is planning time where the new teacher can share ideas with a veteran teacher.
- Set aside times where mentoring teams can visit each other.
- Visit with the teams and ask their opinions on how the program is working; if necessary, make adjustments according to their recommendations.
- Conference with the new teachers and offer your wisdom. Get to know them and make them feel welcomed as an important part of your school.

Chapter Three

Parents and Students

> "Whatever you are,
> be a good one."
> **Abraham Lincoln**

Overview

This chapter deals with concerns that parents may have about school operations, how staff and curriculum affect their child's learning, and how school personnel deal with behavioral and educational issues.

Principals face these topics on an ongoing basis. Articulating the school's goals and finding the right communication tool to address parents and students is not an easy task. Through the snapshots, we will explore the key to communicating solutions, the explanations for why policies are put into effect, and how you may achieve school success by creating an atmosphere where dialoguing with parents and students is an everyday occurrence.

www.schooltalk.com

The Snapshots:

17. Parent Volunteers: Where Are You?
18. Parent Complaint: Teacher Can't Spell
19. The Student Who Continually Says "No."
20. Scheduling Changes: Parent Complaints
21. Parent Is a Pleasure
22. "Look Dick. See Jane." It Was Good Enough for Me
23. A Parent Demands a Grade Change
24. The Student Who Never Writes Anything Down
25. Hold That Thought
26. The Conference That Has No Solution
27. Parent Versus Parent
28. The LEP Dilemma

Snapshot #17:
Parent Volunteers: Where Are You?

Teachers come to you complaining they are not getting any volunteer help from their students' parents, no matter how often they ask or how many flyers they send home. Many parents aren't even signing planners or attending conferences. How should you handle this?

Tip : Have a meeting with teachers to understand their concerns. Get a few to come to another meeting where you invite a few parents in. Together as a team, strategize a plan that can help increase parent volunteerism and the parents' connection to the school. Use the **Parent Involvement Plan Worksheet** *on page 52* to assist you and designate the team members who will be responsible for carrying out the plan.

Provide food and free babysitting at evening events.

Give the parents a "Take-Home Parent Packet" that includes activities parents can do at home with their child(ren).

Parent Involvement Plan Worksheet

Directions: Prior to a "Parent Night," hold a department chair, team, or school improvement meeting. One goal at the meeting can be to develop a plan or guide for parents to do activities at home that match the school's curriculum. What a great way to boost both parents' positive feelings and intensify their commitment to the school and to academic success!

Grade: _____

In-School Curriculum	Ideas to Do At Home

Snapshot #18:

Parent Complaint: Teacher Can't Spell

A parent comes into school, complaining that her child's teacher can't spell. She shows you a note written in her son's daily planner. The teacher wrote that his bringing little toys into school went against her policy, spelling "little" as "liddle." The mother explained she spoke to her son about the problem and that it would never happen again. However, she felt the teacher was wrong as well. Since the woman's son is expected to get a 100 percent on his spelling, why shouldn't the same be expected of the teacher? How should you handle this?

Tip : Thank the parent for bringing this to your attention. Assure her that you feel as strongly as she does about spelling errors and you will speak to the teacher. Call the teacher in and make it clear to her she must be careful when she writes notes to parents whether in planners, letters, or emails. Explain to her that as the teacher, she is the professional and needs to set a good example. Encourage her to always have a dictionary handy, to use spell check, and to check with a colleague when necessary. Remember that written information that goes home or out in the community should always be professional and accurate. Those written communications can achieve positive public relations or can cause great harm to a single staff member or the school.

Use a dictionary and spell check before sending home any flyers and memoranda.

Snapshot #19:
The Student Who Continually Says "No."

David says "No" to all requests from his teacher. His response to doing class assignments is "No." When asked to work on small-group projects, his answer is "No." Even at recess time, he says "No" to going outside. If the teacher insists that he do some of his work, he acts out, throwing books and chairs. The teacher has had it and the parents are just tired of getting notes in the daily planner about their son's behavior. The teacher finally holds a conference and hints that the boy needs to be medicated. The parents are furious. How should you handle this?

Tip : Schedule a meeting with the teacher and the parents. Come up with several options prior to the conference on how best to solve this problem so everyone is satisfied. Listen, talk, and listen some more. From the information the parents give you, try to figure out which option is the right fit. Draw up a behavior contract and reporting system. Remember "teamwork" works. Provide strategies that can be used at school and at home to assist the child with the behaviors. Suggest the teacher keep a journal of behavior and events and give you and the parents a report once a week. Ask the teacher to report the positive as well as the negative events. Plan a follow-up meeting within a reasonable time. Be prepared at that time to review the strategies again. Use all of the resources available to you: the school nurse, counselor, school psychologist, and special teachers.

Report only what you observe, not what you believe. You are not a medical expert.

Snapshot #20:

Scheduling Changes: Parent Complaints

A parent calls you asking why the school wasn't opened the previous night. He had shown up with his son for a seven o'clock meeting to sign up for the school soccer team, only to find the gym locked. Evidently the meeting time had been changed. Now his son has come home from school saying that because he missed the meeting, the coach won't let him be on the team. How should you handle this?

Tip : Tell the parent you are sorry there was a misunderstanding. Assure him you will investigate the situation and get back to him. Get his phone number and ask the best time to reach him. Contact his child's homeroom teacher and the coach. Call them in for a meeting so you can get to the bottom of the situation. Hopefully, you can reach a joint decision on how best to resolve this problem. You don't want to punish the child if the parent was not properly informed. Besides, he may be great at soccer and your team would be losing a terrific player. Call back the parent and present the resolution.

Always make sure any changes to meetings, times, and locations are announced well ahead of time and in several modalities. Announce it on the loud speaker, in a flyer, through the website, on the marquee, and directly to the classes. Make sure all staff is aware of changes as well.

Snapshot #21:

Parent Is a Pleasure

There is one parent who always brings you a cookie or a great cup of coffee. She is always there to help with special functions and loves to plan special events. She truly is a special prize and you couldn't function without her. You wish you could clone her since other parents are not as actively involved. How should you handle this?

Tip : You may want to clone this parent but this is not realistic. Acknowledge that outstanding effort by sharing a smile and sending a note. Utilize this parent to assist you in actively engaging and involving other parents. The best thing you can do is to give her a frequent pat on the back along with a big "thank you." Family-friendly schools increase parent comfort levels, which increases student success. Always recognize the extra efforts that parents make to volunteer.

You can never be too busy for parents who are eager to assist.

Always stroke those who help you out. Everyone needs an occasional "thanks" to keep them smiling and on your side.

Snapshot #22:

"Look Dick. See Jane." It Was Good Enough for Me

Data analysis is the key to student and teacher success.

An irate parent calls with a complaint about the phonics program being taught to his son. He says, "I learned to read 'Look Dick. Look Jane. See Dick. See Jane,' and I am a great reader. I just don't get this push for phonics. My son is struggling and I think this phonetic stuff is for the birds." He demands you make changes immediately. How should you handle this?

Tip : After he calms down, explain to the dad that you would gladly meet with him to discuss the curriculum skills and review recent studies on why the phonics approach is so important to today's learners. This gives you time to gather information; it gives him time to cool down and maybe come to the meeting with a clear head.

Frequent commercials and video games have changed the way children take in information. As teachers, we have to respond to this new way of learning and adjust the way we educate our students. Can we still face an entire group of students, lecture for a half hour, and say, "Now answer the questions in the textbook?"

The delivery of lessons must meet our new generation of learners. We need to entertain, teach, use a variety of teaching styles, and then re-teach. We need to decide whether large-group instruction is appropriate or smaller groups are better. If you remember, *Sesame Street* taught a point, quickly switched to a new concept, and then repeated the lesson. Video games do the same thing, only even faster. We have to teach our educators to be innovative to meet the challenge and to stay ahead of the new learning curves.

57

Snapshot #23:
A Parent Demands a Grade Change

The coach has refused to let his star player, who is failing social studies, continue to play on his team. The rule clearly states, "To play on any school team, a student needs a grade of 'C' or higher in all academic courses, plus all satisfactory or higher marks in 'Effort' for all subject areas." The student's parent is demanding either a grade change on the report card in social studies or that the coach or you bend the rules. His eyes are closed to the fact his son is failing. His focus is the team and so is the student-athlete's. How should you handle this?

Tip :

Call the parent, student, and the coach in for a meeting. Let the coach know ahead of time you are backing him up and you believe a student's academic achievement is more important than his athletic achievement. It may be difficult to stick to this point of view when talking with the parent and student, but you are simply enforcing school policy. You can tell the parent that if the grades improve, his son can participate again but not until then. Sign a contract with the student in which he agrees to bring up his grades. Offer tutoring and assistance, but explain the outcome is up to him.

Reflect on policies at a yearly meeting. Keep the ones that are necessary; change the ones that are not so important.

Snapshot #24:

The Student Who Never Writes Anything Down

During a scheduled conference, a student's parents express concern that their child never gets homework while his friends in the other classes do at least an hour a night. How should you handle this?

Tip : First, assure the parents that the school's policy is to give homework every night, including weekends. Explain that the purpose of the assignments is to let students practice a new skill or to review an old one. It is also an excellent means of informing parents of what exactly is being taught in the classroom. Since you know that the teacher does indeed give homework, call her into the meeting with the student. In a non-threatening manner, open a discussion with the student. You may have the parents lead the conversation. Once it is established that there has been homework and he is not copying it from the board, solutions must be found. A suggestion may be for the student to copy the assignment onto a homework journal. The teacher signs the journal after he copies the assignment, the student signs it to acknowledge he put the right books into his backpack, and the parents initial it every night after they check that the work is complete. Remember to have the teacher make a follow-up phone call to give feedback. Give it a week. Don't wait too long! Think how much that parent will appreciate your interest.

Snapshot #25:

Hold That Thought

A parent comes into your office yelling and screaming that his child is getting picked on by the teacher, has received poor grades, and just hates school. He demands to have the child changed to another classroom or he is going to call the Board of Education about both you and the teacher and tell them how poorly the school is run. How should you handle this?

Tip : During the meeting, let him do all the talking at first. He may simmer down long enough for you to digest all he is saying. Jot down all his important points so you can repeat them when his part of the conversation is complete. This lets him know that you were listening. Try to figure out what the real problem is and work up a solution together. At this point, you may want to bring the student into the meeting. Have a conversation with the student and try to get to the real root of the problem. While you are in the discussion, fill out the **Student Conferencing Worksheet** *on page 61* to assist you in finding out what the student is thinking. Take a good look at the situation. It's possible the student and teacher do not make a good team. There may be an underlying problem you need to resolve. Ask questions and try to work out a solution that would benefit all the parties concerned.

Write down key points and try to understand what the parent is really saying.

Student Conferencing Worksheet

1. Why was the conference called?
☐Review Grades
☐Review Behavior
☐Tardies/Absences
☐Difficulty With Classwork
☐Disagreement With a Grade
☐Late or Missing Class Assignments

2. I learned that my strengths are:
_____
_____
_____
_____
_____

3. I learned that I need to work on:
_____
_____
_____
_____
_____
_____

4. The next marking period, I will improve because I will do the following:
_____
_____
_____
_____
_____
_____
_____

5. Other Comments:
_____
_____
_____
_____
_____
_____

Student's Name: _____
Student's Signature: _____
Administrator's Name: _____
Administrator's Signature: _____
Date: _____

61

Snapshot #26:

The Conference That Has No Solution

A parent comes in, distraught and concerned that this school has not met her child's needs. The child had been retained at her former school and now supposedly is performing below grade level at her new school. The parent has already had several conferences with the teacher, but the child's academic skills have not changed. The student still takes longer than her classmates to learn a new concept and even longer to retain it. The mother can't afford a private tutor. She laments, "Why isn't something being done?" How should you handle this?

Tip : Sit down with the parent to discuss the situation. Explain that the psychologist at the school has met with the school's staff to review her child's grades and portfolio records. The school's personnel feel her child does not meet the criteria to have further testing for a special program. If, after reviewing the documentation, the parent is not convinced and still feels the school is failing her child, stop the conference at this point and reschedule for another day. You may need to bring in the district's specialist to explain the special programs and how the placement works. In the meantime, look for an older student or parent volunteer to work with the child in a small-group or one-to-one setting. Try to set up another conference with the parent to provide resources the parent can do to assist the child at home. Always do what is in the best interest of the student.

Not all conferences have happy endings; you can agree to disagree. Never give up.

Not all conferences work the first time around. Just reschedule and try again. Set a time limit for conferences ahead of time.

Snapshot #27:

Parent Versus Parent

Your secretary tells you a dad she has never seen before has come in to talk to you. He states that he now has custody of his son and the mother cannot come within five hundred feet of the school. He does not offer any proof, such as a copy of any official document. He says he will be back to pick up the child at the regular dismissal time. The office staff is not sure how to handle this situation because the school's file has a copy of a court order designating the mother as the custodial parent and he is not on the pick-up list according to the secretary. How should you handle this?

Tip : Have the front desk staff try to reach the student's mom to alert her of the situation. Tell her that the student will be kept in the principal's office with one of the secretaries until the situation gets cleared up. Call the police to have them assist if there is no officer assigned to the campus. They may be able to assist you in determining whether new court orders were issued and who has the custody rights. Have the police officers stay through dismissal to have clear sailing for the student's sake.

> **You must always obey a court order.**

> **The police can assist when necessary. Remember: the student's safety comes first, not the parents' domestic feud.**

Snapshot #28:
The LEP Dilemma

A parent comes into your office demanding to see you. Realizing that testing is coming soon and her child is way behind, she wants action. She claims her child was labeled Limited English Proficient at her previous school and had accommodations provided. Why hasn't your school done the same? Her threat: Solve this or else I am calling the newspaper and television stations! How should you handle this?

Tip: Pull the child's records. Read them over carefully before you discuss the situation with the parent. Once you know the information, call her in. Listen! Let her vent and then calm her down. Show her the records and explain exactly what is in them. Tell her you would love to help, but at the end of the previous year, the other school had removed her child from the program and he is no longer qualified for any testing accommodations. Pull his academic record and show her his work portfolio. Point out to her the progress her child has made, the areas in which he is strong, and the areas he needs to work on . Offer to follow up with a parent-teacher meeting to see how all the parties concerned can work as a team to help her child succeed.

Be familiar with all federal, state, and local rules and regulations for all special programs.

Points To Ponder:

PONDER
Why engage in a discussion with a very upset parent? Can it ever be successful? Will the child benefit? What do you do?

POINTS
Tips on How to Handle an Unfriendly Parent

1. Smile and thank the parent for coming in. Even though she may expect you to join her in exchanging heated words, remain calm and perhaps even open the discussion with a pleasant story. This may help the parent to simmer down.
2. Listen to the parent and take notes. The parent may have something really important to report to you about her child or the school. Repeat what you hear her say and then redirect the meeting so it becomes constructive instead of destructive.
3. If the parent has only second- or third-hand information, try to get to the source to determine what really happened.
4. Show confidence. While you want to let parents express their feelings, it is your school, so stick to your beliefs and mission. Bend only if you feel it is in the best interest to all the stakeholders.
5. Remember: effective schools run efficiently when there are cooperative teams. Focus on this and not on the negative vibrations of the moment.
6. Remember: not all conferences work. If you're not succeeding in resolving the conflict, get another administrator to help or stop the meeting and try for another time. This allows you to investigate the situation further and, hopefully, the parent will do the same in a calmer and more orderly manner.

PONDER
Teaching a teacher the art of conferencing.

You are asked to sit in on a parent/teacher conference for a child who has not handed in any major assignments. Consequently, the student's grades have plummeted to an F. The teacher knows the parent is quite upset, but the teacher has made several attempts to communicate the problems, without any results. The teacher feels you are needed at the conference because she fears the parent will be hostile and won't listen to what she has to say. What should you do?

POINTS
- Support your staff.
- Get the background on the student.
- Make sure that the teacher is well prepared with the student's portfolio, grades, assignments, and attendance.
- Have the teacher also bring copies of any notes or announcements about rubrics and projects that were sent home with the student.

At the time of the conference:
- Ask the teacher to state only her concerns, not her complaints.
- Let the parent have his say.
- Do not get into an argument with him, or a "he said, she said."
- Don't get defensive, even though he is attacking the teacher's ability to teach and you to lead.
- Try to reach some plan and a conclusion.
- If you can't, end the conference and try again at a later date. If possible, set the date for the follow-up before the parent leaves.

Chapter Four

The Community

"When love and skill
work together, expect
a masterpiece. "
John Ruskin

Overview

Being part of a community is vital. How you, as the school principal, embrace the community—as well as how the community embraces you—is important, and at times, critical to your success.

This chapter deals with working with the community. It discusses ways you can bring the community into the school by communicating and marketing the school and your staff, always keeping in mind the big picture, and that you are there to unite everyone for the good of the cause—the children. It does take a village to raise a child, and to achieve success in today's world, the school and community must be "rowing in the same direction."

The Snapshots:

Snapshot #29:
Handling the Media

Your secretary just received a phone call from the education reporter of your newspaper who wants to interview you on the school's state test scores. You don't know if you should talk to him since you have not received the school's scores yet. You asked your secretary to say you're not available to give you time to think. Should you ignore the phone call or respond? If you respond, what should you say? How should you handle this?

Tip : Never ignore the media. The media has a job to do. They will do it with or without you, so it's in the school's best interest for you to give your help and cooperation. Before you call the reporter back, prepare a script. Write down some key points about your school. What special programs have you implemented to assist the students with the state assessment? What are some of your best practices? If the reporter surprises you with your scores and they are not as high as you expected, be prepared to answer the question: "Why aren't the scores better?" State what you are planning to do for the upcoming school year to assist students who did not meet the state criteria. Whatever you say can be quoted, so be careful with statistics and other important data. Remember, don't talk off the record, because nothing ever is.

Effective communication can lead to many successes.

The mass media can be the vehicle for a positive message.

Snapshot #30:
Positive Partnerships

You have been invited to speak at the local chamber of commerce meeting about the school's current educational programs. The previous principal never participated in any community activity and your secretary tells you she thinks you shouldn't either. How should you handle this?

Tip : Establishing partnerships with community and business organizations brings people into the school who can help on projects, work with teachers and students, and improve student achievement. Go to the meeting and put your best foot forward. Bring along a "brag sheet" of the school's accomplishments and awards received. Be prepared to answer questions and definitely invite all of the members of the chamber to come and take a tour. Your goal is to let everyone know what it takes to run a school, especially on a tight budget. Who knows? You may receive additional resources, donations, or in-kind services to supplement the school. You may even develop a business advocate partner.

Give information about the school in a clear and simple format.

Snapshot #31:

The PTA's Real Agenda

The former PTA president just informed you that the newly elected board had a new agenda in mind. They want parents to have a say in picking their own children's teachers for the upcoming school year. How should you handle this?

Tip : Parents will make requests for specific teachers. Your job, however, is to inform parents that all of your teachers on staff are highly qualified and that teacher selection is done during a team articulation meeting—where the teachers make the assignments with the students' best interest in mind. If the parents persist, have them put in writing the reasons they are requesting a specific teacher. They must be valid and have merit. You may want to meet with those parents who you feel have a legitimate request. Be careful. Be fair. You do not want to start something that may be hard to control later.

Ask all committees and parent groups to give you an agenda prior to their scheduled meeting.

Snapshot #32:

Too Good to Be True

A vendor calls wanting to donate $5,000.00 worth of software and books to the school's media center. You can't believe your luck until he mentions that he also wants to hold an essay-writing contest for the students. But, there's more—the parents would need to fill out a permission slip including their name, address, and phone number. The vendor promises to send the software and books as soon as he gets all of the permission slips back. How should you handle this?

Tip:

Be careful. As the school's educational leader, you are an agent of the school board and trusted by parents and you do not want to betray this trust. What is the vendor's true agenda? Why does he need the parents to give permission to the students if this is a writing contest? Vendors are becoming savvier. The vendor may be doing his job and this may be legitimate, but before you approve anything, do your homework. Ask for a list of schools within the district that are participating in this contest. Call other principals and talk to them about this program. Ask questions. Is the contest a district sponsored event? Ask your teachers if they want their students to participate. It is better to be safe than sorry.

Research any program before it is implemented.

Snapshot #33:
New Building

The community is outraged that the new building being built at the school will bring an additional 500 students. Traffic is bad enough as it is without this. You have received several phone calls and several irate neighbors have come to the school already. The situation is getting hotter by the day. How should you handle this?

Tip : With the help of district personnel and community leaders, have a meeting to discuss concerns. Be careful though—you don't want to be the target of a lynch mob. Call the city and ask for the person who handles traffic patterns. See if she can assist you in coming up with solutions to the traffic problem. Making streets one-way during certain times might possibly help alleviate traffic concerns. Another solution is staggering the arrival and dismissal times of the students. Have a plan—stick to an agenda and allow the people to discuss their concerns. The focus should always be what's best for the students while keeping the needs of the community close at hand.

Plan ahead to avoid problem situations.

Snapshot #34:
To Join or Not to Join

One of the parents at your school calls and invites you to become a member of the local chamber of commerce. He has just been elected to the board and wants to have you involved with the education committee. You are concerned about this added responsibility to your already limited time. You are hesitant to reply. How should you handle this?

Tip: By all means join. The local chamber of commerce is a great way to market and showcase the school. You also are being asked to sit on a very important committee for this organization. Take advantage of this opportunity to establish partnerships and expand your network with others in the community. If time is limited, you may want to also involve another staff member to sit in for you when you are unable to attend. You should be honored that you have been selected to participate on the education committee. Your involvement is important as well as your input.

The community needs you.

Snapshot #35:

Public Relations

One of your teachers was arrested and charged with a DUI. It was reported in the local paper and now everywhere you go you are stopped and asked about the incident. How should you handle this?

Tip : Never discuss confidential information about an incident with anyone outside of those people who are directly involved. When you are asked, politely state that you are unable to discuss this while an investigation is ongoing. Assure the person asking that the school is running smoothly and that the safety of the students is first and foremost, as always. Remember our system of justice presumes innocence until guilt is proven. However, there may be school board rules or special programs, such as an "Employee Assistance Program" that you should consider in your school-site actions.

Avoid the rumor mill. Confidentiality must be maintained.

Snapshot #36:
Lockdown Mode

A call comes in from a distraught parent stating that two armed robbers just shot out the windows to a jewelry store that's only five blocks away from your school. The men are on the run. You can hear the police sirens roaring in the background. How should you handle this?

Tip : Thank the parent and immediately implement a lockdown. Your faculty and staff should have procedures and know what to do. Call the police to verify this rumor and to inform them of your actions. If you do not have a police officer at your school, you should request one. They may already be on their way. This will assist you in providing added security to the school during this emergency situation. Assign a person in the main office to handle all parent phone calls; make sure that you write a script for them to use. Parents who come to the school to pick up their children should be directed to a waiting area. However, keep in mind their safety is also at risk. Your number one priority is to keep the students, faculty, and staff safe.

Meet with the local police each year to design or update an emergency plan. Share this plan with the faculty during your first meeting.

To make sure that everyone knows what to do conduct safety drills on an ongoing basis. Have a written plan with stated procedures. Give the plan to everyone at the school and practice, practice, practice. Make certain that everyone including secretaries, custodians, and food service workers practice the procedures and know what to do in case of an emergency.

Snapshot #37:

A Special Request

A prominent community leader just called and informed you that he wants you to register his child at your school. However, because this family does not live in your area, doing so would go against district policy. How should you handle this?

Tip : Always follow procedures and policies. Inform the community leader that you would be thrilled to have his son at your school, but he must obtain a transfer to do so. Assist him in the process. Let him know where to go, who to talk to, and how long it takes. No matter who may ask you for a favor, it is always best to stick to the rules. You can facilitate and provide assistance, but you can't change policy.

Violating a policy is not a good idea.

Points To Ponder:

PONDER

How do you become an effective communicator and spread the good news of the school?

POINTS

Proper listening is a communication skill that creates a positive acceptance for understanding, affirmation, validation, and appreciation. As the educational leader, you need to communicate with all school stakeholders, even those that may seem less than enthusiastic that you are the principal. Your listening will elicit a better response from your students, parents, faculty and staff, school board members, and community leaders than simply talking at them—something we do without much thought. Make sure that you:

- Warmly greet and smile at everyone who comes your way.
- Never lock yourself behind closed doors.
- Be visible and accessible.
- Understand the needs of all school stakeholders.
- Encourage positive rewards with notes and telephone calls.

- Say "thank you" to those who give assistance and go beyond their duties.
- Create an atmosphere of involvement.
- Be a mentor.
- Participate in community happenings.
- Create a school atmosphere that encourages everyone to be their best.

PONDER

What is the best way to deal with the media?

POINTS

When dealing with the media:

- Be prepared.
- Speak slowly.
- Listen and reflect on what you are saying.
- If you don't want to be quoted, don't say it.
- Remember, nothing is OFF the record.
- Use *Communicating With the Media on page 130* to assist you.

Notes: _____

Notes:

Chapter Five

Smooth Operations

> "When written in Chinese, the word 'crisis' is composed of two characters. One represents danger and the other represents opportunity."
> **John F. Kennedy**

Overview

The smooth operation of the school is crucial to your success. A leader who is organized and has established procedures and routines has done much to set the tone for the success of the school. This chapter deals with positive communications that set the tone for a successful school day and a successful school year.

The Snapshots:

Snapshot #38:
First Day of School Sets the Tone

Last year, the first day of school was very chaotic. Even though you put up class lists early that morning, parents still had a difficult time finding their way around. You had no time to greet returning students or talk to the teachers. You want things to run more smoothly this year. How should you handle this?

Tip: The very first day of school sets the tone for the year. What is the best roadmap to have ready? Consider having a school orientation day. Designate the day before the first day of school as a special orientation day where parents and students can come in and tour the school, check to see where the classroom is, and meet briefly with the teacher. Have a welcome packet with a map of the school. The more specific the activity or event the less chance of chaos. Many schools have organized activities specifically for this purpose. You may want to set a time and plan specific activities that will make this a positive encounter for the student, teacher, and parent. Check the organization called "The First Day of School Foundation" for an activity guide, video, and ideas as to what other schools are doing across the country. Their website is http://www.firstday.org. You may want to enlist the assistance of teachers, the PTA, and community.

> You are the educational leader; set the tone for a successful year by getting off to a great start.

Snapshot #39:

Hiring Staff

You have a teaching position opening up. You have advertised the position and you are ready to interview. On the day of the interviews, a school board member calls you with a special request: One of her family members is a teacher and she wants you to hire her in this position. How should you handle this?

Tip: Let the board member know your school has an interview committee that interviews and selects the candidates. Ask that her family member contact you to schedule a day and time to interview.

You should have an interview committee at the school; if not, set one up. The committee should consist of the principal, or the assistant principal; the grade-level or department chairperson for the position being interviewed; and two additional teachers. If you are in a public school system with a teachers' union or association, one of those teachers should be the steward of the school. If you are in a private or other type of school you may want to have someone from your board on the committee. Before the interview, prepare three or four questions with the assistance of the committee. Give each member of the committee a question to ask. A favorite questions is: "Why do you feel you are the best person for this position?" Notice the response the person gives; listen to what is not said as much as what is said. You may want to select three finalists to come back for another level of interviews before your final selection is made. You can do this with any position that becomes open at your school. Call the school board member back, even if it is with bad news. You should explain the committee's decision, based on what is in the best interest of the school.

Always treat everyone equally and fairly.

Snapshot #40:
Good Morning

Your new media specialist/librarian, who was assigned to your school, wants nothing to do with CCTV (closed circuit television) operation in the media center, saying she feels it is not part of her responsibilities. Your former media specialist/librarian, who retired last year, ran the entire operation. With your sophisticated equipment and a group of dedicated students who acted as the crew, she produced a short news show every morning about the upcoming day's events. As the principal you feel this is a positive way to start the school day. The staff and student body look forward to the broadcast and the students love to work as the crew. This has become an issue. What should you do?

It is always a good idea to have several staff members in the school trained to do crucial functions so that there is always someone on staff who knows what to do.

Tip : From the time the first school bell rings until the end of the school day, procedures and routines are necessary to set the tone for the smooth operation of the school. First and foremost, make sure to go over what a new employee's responsibilities will be. As the media specialist, she should be in charge of everything in the media center. Possibly she does not know how to handle the equipment and may need to get training. In the meantime you have to run the school smoothly. If the staff and students have always relied on the morning show to start their day, you need to arrange for it to continue. Consider all of your resources. See whether the former media specialist/librarian is available to come and train her successor and another staff member. Check to see whether another school in the area can send its trained staff member to train yours. Discuss the issue with the new media specialist/librarian. Are you willing to relinquish this as one of her duties and responsibilities and give it to another one of your staff members? You may decide that you want her to run this program and if she does not, you will have to take appropriate action.

Snapshot #41:

Building a Positive School Community

You have so many activities going on daily at the school along with meetings, district projects, and grade-level assessments, your staff finds it difficult to keep track of what is due, what meetings are going on, and who is out of the building. How should you handle this?

Tip : Building a positive school community is important, and the best way to do this is through communications. Many times, the amount of work, timelines, and commitments become overwhelming. The best way to communicate and keep the staff informed is by delivering a bulletin for the upcoming week to every staff member's mailbox on the Friday before that week begins. Break down the days of the week and note meetings (including time and place), special testing, paperwork due, and other important information in this bulletin. You can also note resources available for the teachers, motivational quotes, birthdays, and important reminders. To maintain a cohesive school community, always place the mission statement or your theme at the top of the bulletin. A weekly bulletin, targeted to the faculty and staff, will keep everyone informed and contribute to the smooth operations. Give the faculty and staff a procedure where they can contribute their important dates and events for the school bulletin.

Weekly staff bulletins keep everyone informed and on track.

Snapshot #42:

The Master Schedule

At an elementary school's general PTA meeting, a parent raises her hand and asks why the students don't have physical education every day. The question immediately stirs up the crowd and more parents add their voices, many becoming upset. "That's why our kids are fat!" yells another one. How should you handle this?

If meetings become heated, it is always best to table the issue and have a separate meeting to discuss it.

Know your curriculum requirements.

Tip : Every state and school district has different curriculum requirements. Do your due diligence and know what they are. In this school district, the "recommended" minimum requirement was two hours per week for second through fifth grades. The principal, as the educational leader, created the school's master schedule, which consisted of a one-hour block of time twice a week for students in these grade levels. What did the principal do to address this issue? She informed the parents of the requirements and the reasons why the school had adopted a one-hour block of time twice a week. Master schedules are just like pieces of a puzzle that must interlock and match to get a complete picture. The components consist of students, curriculum, site plan, classroom teachers, and auxiliary staff. Tackling a master schedule is never an easy task. For the visual learners, there are erasable boards designed just for scheduling. They usually come in different sizes and you will need magnets in many colors to designate grades, courses, electives, and/or teachers. This tool definitely helps to cut down on all the pencil-and-paper mistakes.

The first step is to determine state and district guidelines, curriculum standards, and required courses, along with the minimum time requirements. Establish set sections or classes, based on teacher availability and student enrollment. Determine classes according to the school's philosophy and mission. Continue to communicate with the data processor and registrar to maintain the ratios that are needed for each class.

Remember, as principal, you should have the final say on all scheduling decisions since you will be the one receiving the phone calls if anything goes wrong. Consider the teacher preference and certification for grade-level assignments, the number of students entering each grade, the capacity of children per room, the location of the rooms, and the need to meet high academic expectations. If your explanation does not satisfy their concerns, refer this issue to the school advisory committee. The committee can then study the issue and bring the alternatives to the parents. The bottom line is that another part of the curriculum would have to be cut to add more physical education classes. If this is not possible, consider giving the parents suggestions on how to increase their children's physical activity at home.

Snapshot #43:

The Family Feud

Surveys are a great way to understand what needs to be adjusted or kept the same.

You have just been appointed principal of a school. In the first few weeks, you notice many of the faculty and staff have negative attitudes and low morale. There is also a high rate of faculty absenteeism and turnover. You realize you need to change this quickly before it gets worse. How should you handle this?

Tip : First, survey the faculty and staff—the best and most expedient way to learn about issues at the school site. You may find that you will gain more information through a survey than by having a staff meeting. Let the respondents complete the survey anonymously so they feel free to express their true feelings without fear of repercussions. Use the **Anonymous Staff Survey** *on page 89*. After obtaining the results of the survey, schedule small informal brainstorming meetings to address the issues identified and to work out solutions. You may want to consider scheduling these meetings throughout the grade levels or departments.

Before each meeting, set the ground rules and select a moderator to keep the group on task. Put the issues in order of priority, then brainstorm. As the instructional leader and captain of the ship, you want to show your staff you are willing to work with them in a cooperative and positive way. After you have met with the entire faculty and staff, set a date for a general meeting for all to attend at which you can present the results of the survey, the issues at hand, and the recommendations discussed. At this large meeting, you may want to divide the group into smaller groups for further discussion and planning. The goal is to get the staff openly talking together and coming up with recommendations in a non-threatening environment. Set the tone, be positive, and provide a forum for good communication. A key to your success in building morale is to allow teachers to provide ideas and implement them. You may not be able to turn the school around in a day or a week, but at least the staff will know you are sensitive to their needs.

Anonymous Staff Survey

Please respond to each question below. You do not need to sign your name, unless you would like us to respond to a specific concern you have. The purpose of the survey is to encourage faculty and staff to communicate freely and candidly about issues facing our school.

We appreciate your time and effort. Thank you.

What are the areas that need to be addressed at the school?
_____
_____

What is working?
_____
_____

What should be done differently?
_____
_____

What would you do to make the school better?
_____
_____
_____
_____

List important needs of the school in order of priority.
1. _____
2. _____
3. _____
4. _____
5. _____
6. _____

How can the principal best support you in meeting the needs of the students?
_____
_____
_____

What do you believe we should do to make our school more successful?
_____
_____
_____

Snapshot #44:
On the Same Page

The end of the year is coming to a close and the teachers are already complaining. They are concerned about next school year's grade-level and classroom assignments, expectations, and overall accountability. You have tried to address this at the general faculty meeting, but have not been successful because of several "vocal and negative" staff members. How should you handle this?

Tip:

As the instructional leader, you must have a vision and keep that vision alive in everyone's eyes. It's also essential to have your faculty and staff on your side. The best way to bring about consensus is to have planning meetings where all staff is involved and everyone shares ideas and brings forth recommendations to make the upcoming year even better. Start your planning meetings small, throughout each grade level/department. Provide surveys and questionnaires to get the process started. Designate the grade-level or department chairperson to bring back recommendations and results. Then have a planning meeting with all grade-level/department chairpersons, which means the entire faculty and staff will be represented and everyone has a chance to participate. This will allow you to plan for the upcoming school year in a timely manner and keep up-to-date on the needs and the recommendations of the staff. Use the **Planning Meeting for the Upcoming School Year Worksheet** *on page 91* to assist you. Remember, the key to a principal's success is a staff that is successful.

> *One of the keys to being an effective principal is to consistently monitor the practices that have been put in place to achieve student, staff, and school success. You want to have the teachers participate actively in this process.*

Planning Meeting for the Upcoming School Year Worksheet

"If one does not know to which port is sailing, no wind is favorable."
SENECA

As we begin to close the year, I would like for each and every one of you to reflect individually, and then collectively begin conversations on the following:

• What really worked for you this year?
• What instructional program was "above the top" for you and the students?
• What would you like to see implemented at the school?
• How can the support services of the school assist you, your students, and the grade-level or department better?
• What do we need to work on to improve or fine tune our successes?
• Where do we go from here?
• What is our vision for the future?

Please discuss these items and others you feel are important at your next grade-level/department meeting. The grade-level and department chairpersons will be meeting with you next month to begin to plan for the upcoming school year. Your participation is important!

Snapshot #45:

Budget

You have received phone calls from several concerned parents. They want you to hire teacher aides to assist teachers in the classroom. You know you have no money in the school budget to do this. However, they are very insistent. How should you handle this?

Tip : First let the parents know that even though you currently have no money in the school budget to fund teacher aides, you are willing to consider other ways and options to satisfy their request. Look at some creative ways to do this, such as writing a grant proposal specifically for teacher aides in the classroom. Do you have a PTA that is willing to assist you in funding this request? Look at other ways and means to fund this important request and work with the faculty, staff, and parents to do what is best for the students. Do you currently have part-time or hourly employees who can be shared to meet this need? Explore creative ways with parents to address this very important request.

Utilize all resources.

Snapshot #46:
State Certified

Your special education teacher just informed you that she was leaving the school. You have three weeks before school begins to find someone to replace her, but there is no one with her certification available. How should you handle this?

Tip : Immediately contact your school district or state department of education office and find out if there are any exceptions given for a principal in your situation. If they do not allow exceptions, and you still cannot find a state-certified teacher, find out what other options you may have.

What can you do to fill the spot where there is a teaching need? Do an investigation and find out if your state waives certification on an emergency basis provisionally for a teacher. States define their certification requirements in their state laws, rules, and regulations. In some situations, states have allowed alternative methods of certification, especially in certification areas that are hard to find. Some states allow a teacher to be fully certified as long as she passes a subject area test. Find out your options quickly and try to get a teacher hired before the first day of school. You may survey your staff to see if someone is already certified but teaching something else and wants a change in assignment.

> *Know your state certification requirements and any allowable exceptions.*

93

Snapshot #47:

Teacher Support

Last year you hired three beginning teachers who you thought were top-notch. They impressed the staff and interviewed well. However, they ended up performing far below expectations. In fact one of them left during the middle of the school year. It is hard enough to find teachers, let alone good ones. How should you handle this?

Tip : Providing a support system for new teachers is critical to their success and that of the school. This year start by teaming each of these teachers with one of your best teachers. Orient them in the school's way of doing things. Set high expectations for them and provide opportunities for their professional development. Many districts now offer induction programs to assist new teachers. Find out if your school system has any such programs and get these teachers help immediately. Remember, you have valuable experience to share and so does your veteran staff. Share your wisdom on: classroom management, curriculum instruction, lesson planning, and best practices. If your interview/selection process is not identifying highly qualified teachers, you may need to review it and make appropriate revisions.

Continuously monitor what goes on in each classroom to avoid surprises.

Snapshot #48:

Accounting for Accountability

The state test scores just arrived at school and you are eager to see how well the school did as a whole as well as how the individual students did. Before you give out the results, you want to analyze the data. How should you handle this?

The center of all activity in schools is teaching and learning. Are your teachers teaching and your students learning?

Don't wait for the end of the year to analyze data. It is an ongoing process.

Tip: Disseminating the data is important. As the instructional leader, you need to know what is happening in the classrooms. Ask yourself: Is quality instruction taking place? One of the best gauges of this is to conduct an assessment of data. When you have this in place, review with each faculty member how his or her class did as a whole on each skill. Discuss with them how they might bring up student performance for the following year. Track the progress throughout the year to ensure a high-quality curriculum and good results prior to the standardized testing date. By analyzing the data, examining the test scores, and keeping a record of individualized student gains, you can make adjustments to strategies and instructional programs to ensure that students are meeting the curriculum goals that are expected. Assessments are given to measure student learning. If schools are to improve, educators must measure growth of student achievement. An effective leader knows how to use assessments to gauge what's working and what isn't, and then provide accommodations and improvements where necessary. Such tests enable you to know where and how to fine-tune your organization and improve the instructional program.

Snapshot #49:

Easy Money

You have recognized a burning issue at your school that warrants attention. Several students who are not reading on grade level would benefit greatly from small-group tutoring. You have no additional monies to fund this program but feel passionately that this would give those students the boost they need. How should you handle this?

Tip : Grants are great ways to secure monies for programs that otherwise may not be funded. Do a search on the Internet or call your district or state department of education office and find out what grants are readily available. Convene a committee of teachers that are interested in this special program and work out a grant-writing plan. Districts may have a grant office where additional information and grant-writing tips can be obtained. No matter how small the amount of the grant, it is a great way to secure programs and resources. Find out the resources available to you. You may also approach the PTA or business partners for help.

Be resourceful.

Grant writing is an art. Send staff to grant-writing workshops or go to one yourself.

Snapshot #50:

Open the Door

The principal before you had a "closed-door policy." She was never available to others and projected the attitude of "I am the boss." Teachers had left the school in large numbers; those teachers who remained were very uninvolved in the school. The teaching climate was awful. How should you handle this?

Tip : Elicit remaining staff to assist in making changes and mentoring the newcomers. Let them become "your team." Word will travel quickly that things are changing for the positive. Like weather, school climates can change; make yourself available to your staff. Hold meetings and let staff share in the decision-making process. Create a positive environment for teachers by bringing in treats and providing a "thank you" when appropriate. Start a social committee and designate a special night for teachers to meet and socialize.

A positive and caring atmosphere is essential to a smoothly run school.

An open-door policy for staff, parents, and students can create a positive school climate and encourage harmony.

Snapshot #51:

Your School Is Part of the Community

The Parks and Recreation Department for the city needs a field for soccer play. Your school has the perfect one. You get a call and are asked to provide time on the field for the soccer team. How should you handle this?

Tip : Invite the person in charge of the Parks and Recreation Department to come to the school for a meeting. Discuss their needs as well as yours. See how you can come to a compromise to help the kids on the soccer team. Make sure the team's practice will not interfere with the operations of the school and will be conducted at a time convenient for your school and student body. Is there a "Use of Building" form that needs to be signed? Make sure that you cover all of the legal points and get everything in writing. Do your best to make this a win-win situation for everyone. Determine who will supervise the activities and who will be responsible for the safety of the children. Make sure that there will be a sufficient number of adults to supervise.

> **Know the policies and procedures to follow when outside agencies use your facility.**

Snapshot #52:
Paint Job

The school is in need of a paint job. The classroom walls are dingy and the paint on the exterior of the building is peeling. You choose the colors and contact the district to put in a request for painting. Everything is a "go" until you get a phone call and find out that the city must approve the exterior colors. You really want to go ahead with the painting. What should you do?

Tip : Always do your homework. Many cities have very strict guidelines. Even though some schools and school districts may fall outside of the city codes, it is best to work positively with everyone involved. Immediately call the painters and stop the project. Get a sample of the colors you have chosen for the school and call the city to schedule a meeting where you can present them. Listen and try to work within the parameters imposed by the city while still serving the needs of your school. Many times you will be surprised at the outcome.

Schools need to be good neighbors too.

Know maintenance procedures.

Points To Ponder:

PONDER
The hiring of highly qualified teachers is a critical process to a high-quality, successful school. What should you look for in a résumé? Remember the resume is not as important as the interview and both not as important as the actual performance.

POINTS
The following are points to consider when reading a resume.

- Goals are clear.
- Addresses and contact information are visible.
- Experiences are listed in order, starting from the present.
- No unexplained gaps exist between jobs listed on the time line.
- Text is easy to read and follow.
- Statements show applicant is a team player.
- Special achievements stated are relevant to the job.
- Writing is error free.
- Experiences listed are in the same field as that of the job for which the applicant is applying.
- References are listed and are job related.
- List of teaching qualifications and documents are included.

PONDER
As the educational leader, what are the qualities and characteristics of a good teacher mentor?

POINTS
Good mentors:

- Can work on a collaborative team.
- Know the curriculum.
- Employ strategies to teach effectively.
- Are experienced.
- Have received excellent evaluations for a minimum of three consecutive years.
- Communicate well.
- Exhibit confidentiality.
- Enjoy an excellent rapport with parents and colleagues.
- Understand the mission and the philosophy of the school.
- Have shown leadership qualities.
- Are respected by colleagues.
- Like to share ideas.
- Are flexible.
- Can multi-task.
- Are supportive.

Notes : _____

H ow do others see you? It takes courage to be willing to listen and make changes based on others' opinions of you. If you are not ready to venture on this journey just yet, you may want to ask one of your most trusted friends for an honest opinion.

We would like to leave you with these final thoughts . . . Have you ever encountered a situation where you were talking to someone, but not getting your point across . . . or you felt as though you were speaking in a foreign language, because your listener clearly did not understand what you were trying to say? Remember, you hold within yourself the key to effective communication. Only you have the power to communicate your thoughts and ideas to others—no one else can do this for you. The good news is that anyone who is willing to make some changes and has the determination to succeed can master this essential skill. You will find when you change your communication techniques and style for the better, your listeners will react accordingly.

We want you to be effective in all your communications. By using the information we share in this book, you can approach any situation that requires good communication skills with confidence. May you continue your journey of communicating effectively with everyone who crosses your path. The more you practice the tools and techniques provided here, the better communicator you will become. By communicating effectively, you will not only serve your own needs, you will be better equipped to serve those of your students and their parents.

We send our best wishes for your continued growth from every communication opportunity that comes your way. We would love to hear from you! How did the book help you, what were your favorite snapshots, and which tips or worksheets did you like best? Please send us your comments.

You can write to us at:

Cheli Cerra
9737 N.W. 41 Street, #356
Miami, FL 33178
Cheli@school-talk.com

Ruth Jacoby
P. O. Box 8405
Coral Springs, FL 33075
DrRuth@school-talk.com

We look forward to effectively communicating with You!

Share Your Snapshots

Your Snapshot

How do you make communication easier?

We invite you to share with us your snapshots. Please let us know what situations you have dealt with, what tools you have developed, and what worksheets you use to make your communications easier. We would love to feature you in our next book.

Please send submissions to:
submissions@school-talk.com

You can also visit the school-talk.com website at **http://www.school-talk.com** or personally email each author at the address below:
Cheli at: Cheli@school-talk.com
Ruth at: DrRuth@school-talk.com

We hope that you have enjoyed reading ***Principal Talk!*** as much as we have enjoyed writing it.

Appendix A
Stress Buster Tips and Sample Letters

Attendance

Date:_____

Dear Parent(s) of_____,
Child's Name

Here at _____we are committed to having our children
Name of School
excel in all areas of the school program. It is our belief that regular attendance is an
important contributor to a student's high performance.

We need your support. There are legitimate reasons your child may miss a day of school, one
being if there is an illness. However, we hope you will make every effort to have your child
attend every day. If your child is late, it's better to receive a tardy than to miss an entire day
of school.

Thank you.

Sincerely,

Principal

Class Assignments

Date:_____

Dear Mr. and Mrs. Parent,

I received your letter requesting a change in class assignment for your child, _____.
I understand your concerns and issues.

After speaking with your child's teacher and reviewing his portfolio, which included samples of his work, report cards, and test scores, I see no reason for a reassignment at this time.

He is doing proficient work in his academic areas and is presenting great effort in class. His assignments are handed in on time with limited errors. His teacher feels that with additional praise and encouragement, his understanding of concepts will continue to improve.

If you would like to conference with me or the teacher, please feel free to call and make an appointment. I look forward to meeting with you to discuss any areas of concerns, so that we can come to an agreement on how best to help _____.

As always, thank you for your continued support.

Sincerely,

Principal

Congratulations

Date:_____

Dear Mr. and Mrs. Support,

I take great pleasure on letting you know that your child, _____, has made the A Honor Roll for this grading period. I am thrilled to share this great accomplishment with you. This is certainly a milestone in your child's academic life.

It is truly a reflection on how hard he has worked in school and at home. With supportive parents like yourselves, such goals can be achieved.

I am looking forward to seeing you at our Honor Roll Assembly on April 13th.

Best Wishes.

Sincerely,

Principal

On Notice

Date: _____

To the Parent(s) of _____ ,

This is to inform you that, as of this grading period, your child has not shown proficiency in the following subject areas:

_____

_____

_____

_____

Please call to set up a conference with your child's teacher(s) to see how, as a team, we all can assist your child in improving his or her grade(s). There still may be time to turn that failing grade into a passing one. If this does not happen, your child may need to repeat the grade.

Sincerely,

Principal

Meet the Teacher
Announcing Open House

Dear (School Name) Parents,

We'd like to invite you to attend our Open House, September 12th, from 6:30 to 8:30 P.M.

We feel it is so important for parents to meet their child's teacher(s) at the beginning of the school year. You will learn about the school and the classroom rules and policies. Your questions regarding policies on dress code, homework, grading, textbooks, and curriculum will be answered, and you will have the opportunity to visit and learn about your child's school environment.

This is also the time to get your questions answered and to learn all about our expectations for your child this school year. You will be able to look at all the textbooks and instructional materials to be used, review the schedule, and enjoy some of your child's work that has been completed during these first days of school.

The staff and faculty are looking forward to making this the best school year yet. We hope to see you at the Open House.

Sincerely,

(School Name) Staff

Volunteer Thank You

Date: _____

Dear Mrs. Cheerful,

I know that when you came into my office and said you would love to help, you never thought I would give you such a tremendously time-consuming task. I did so because I knew you could do it and do it well.

Thank you so much for making our Third Annual Book Sale such a huge success. Because of your dedication and ability to get so many others to help out, we raised more money than we anticipated and far outreached our goal. We have used the funds to extend our school library and computer lab.

Students and staff alike will enjoy many hours of reading pleasure and have access to new sources of information thanks to the books and computer software we were able to purchase.

Again, I extend my gratitude for everything that you and your team accomplished. You have allowed us to create a legacy of learning that will last for years to come.

Sincerely,

Principal

Student Accomplishment

Date: _____

Student's Name: _____

This letter is to inform you that you have made the HONOR ROLL for this grading period. As principal I want to congratulate you on all the hard work and effort you have shown your teachers and parents.

I am so proud to add your name to the list of special students at our school and look forward to handing to you your Certificate of Merit next week at our assembly.

Keep up the good work!

Sincerely,

Principal

Behavior Reflection

Name: _____

Class: _____

Date: _____

Today, I was sent to the office because:

_____
_____
_____
_____
_____
_____

The school/class rule that I chose not to follow was:

_____
_____
_____
_____
_____

I should have done the following so I would not be writing this paper:

_____
_____
_____

My parents' reaction will be:

_____
_____
_____
_____
_____

My teacher's reaction was:

_____
_____
_____
_____
_____

My classmates' reactions were:

_____
_____
_____
_____
_____
_____

Student's Signature: _____
Teacher's Signature: _____
Parent's Signature: _____

Welcome Back Letter to Teachers

Date: _____

Dear: _____

The school bell is ready to ring. "Welcome Back" to another great year! The administration has been busy planning for another successful academic year, plus a year full of wonderful activities for you, your students, and parents.

Yes, the summer did go by swiftly and I do hope you have come back with new ideas and are geared up to share them with your colleagues and students. The books and materials are waiting to be opened and explored.

Every year is a challenge. We have always met them and succeeded. This year we are implementing the new curricula that you decided upon at our last meeting in June.

I know we are in for a wonderful adventure and a dynamic year ahead.

Good Luck!

Principal

Open House "Thank You"

Date: _____

Dear: _____

The complimentary phone calls have not stopped since our very successful Open House!

Thanks to the teachers, paraprofessionals, and food service and custodial staff for making the parents feel like this school is truly a second home for their children. The secretaries have been busy writing down all the comments, and I will share them with you in the statements below.

First impressions are the most important. All of you put your best foot forward and it showed. Thank you for your dedication and for going that "extra mile" that makes our school stand far above the rest. I am continually telling people I meet that the faculty and staff at our school are the best. Our successful Open House is just another example of how true that is.

Sincerely,

Principal

Below are several testimonials from parents:
"The teacher was warm and had the best smile."
"I now know why your school believes in homework."
"The new textbooks look great."
"The building is so much cleaner this year."

Please Help–Publicity Is Our Best PR

Dear Teachers,

I always welcome information about something outstanding that you have done with your students or something stupendous one of your students has accomplished. Sometimes your team does an exciting art project or research project or even a character education activity.

I want you to know and I want our community to know what a great job you are doing with our students. If you have something to share, please give me samples and take photos so I can then pass the information on to the news media.

Thank you so much.

Sincerely,
Miss Hospitality

Project: _____
Teacher: _____
Class: _____
Students: _____
Date: _____

Brief description and history of why this project was done:
_____
_____
_____
_____

Model and Talent Release Form

I hereby give the school board and its employees, agents, licensees, representatives, or assigns, and those acting under their permission and upon their authority or those for whom the school district is acting, the absolute right and permission to copyright and/or use and/or publish, exhibit, display, broadcast, or print any portions of films, videotapes, kinescopes, audiotapes, still pictures, slides, or any other type of recording in which I may be included in whole or part, made through any media, without inspection or approval of the finished product or use to which it may be applied.

I also grant the right to include my possessions and/or background objects which may appear in the final product.

I further release the school board and its representatives, assigns, agents, or licensees from any liability for what I or anyone claiming by, through, or under me might deem misrepresentations or in connection with use of any of the aforementioned items in which I may have appeared. I am 18 years of age or older and have read the above authorization and release prior to its execution. If under 18 years of age, legal guardian indicated below has signed on my behalf.

Print Name:_____

Signature:_____

Address:_____

Witness: _____

SIGNATURE OF PARENT OF GUARDIAN, IF UNDER 18 YEARS OF AGE

Signature of Parent/Guardian:_____

Address of Parent/Guardian:_____

It's Time for Observations

Date: _____

Dear: _____

I will be conducting teacher observations beginning on _____ .
This is your first formal observation for this school year. It will be approximately thirty minutes long. I
would like to see a reading or mathematics lesson.

Please have your lesson plan book on your desk, along with your weekly plans. I will be looking at grade
books and reviewing content of student portfolios. Please make sure the plans include your objectives,
curriculum goals, LEP strategies, benchmarks, procedures, and evaluative measurements. I would also
like to see what follow-up lessons and homework instructions you will give to your students after this
lesson is completed. I will be looking at classroom management styles and bulletin boards, as well as
delivery of the lesson and lesson content.

Please fill in the bottom survey sheet and return to my secretary by the end of the day tomorrow.

Sincerely,

Principal

Teacher's Name: _____ **Class:** _____
Date: _____
Time: _____ **A.M.** _____ **P.M.**

Substitute Report

Please fill out and return to the main office secretary at the end of the day. Don't forget to sign in and out.

Name: _____

Date: _____

Teacher you substituted for:
_____

Lessons you taught: _____
_____

Math: _____
_____

Reading: _____
_____

Language Arts: _____
_____

Creative Writing: _____
_____

Science: _____
_____
_____

Social Studies: _____
_____

Other: _____
_____

Homework Given: _____
_____

Absent Student(s): _____
_____

Tardy Student(s): _____
_____

Behavior Concerns: _____
_____

Student Helper(s): _____
_____

Thank you for serving as a substitute today. Can we call you again? _____
What is the best way to reach you? _____
_____

A Job Well Done

Date: _____

Dear: _____

Thank you so much for the school play you put on for your grade-level team. The proud looks on the parents' faces and the smiles on all the students in the audience told me that your goal to entertain and to give a message was very well received. I, too, enjoyed watching the students perform. I especially liked the costumes the students made with the help of their parents.

Thank you for volunteering and for contributing of so much of your time.

Your assistance and your enthusiasm are greatly appreciated. As always, you did a exemplory job.

Thank you so much.

Sincerely,

Principal

Grade-level/Team Meetings Minutes Form

Meeting Date: _____

Staff Present: _____
_____
_____
_____

Staff Absent: _____
_____
_____
_____

Agenda:
1. _____
2. _____
3. _____
4. _____
5. _____
6. _____
7. Other _____

Ideas Generated: _____
_____
_____
_____
_____

Area of Concerns: _____
_____
_____
_____
_____

Suggestions Made: _____
_____
_____
_____
_____

Dates to Save: _____
_____
_____
_____
_____

Next Meeting: _____
_____
_____
_____

127

The Interview Process

Step-by-Step

Interviews are important and should be shared by a team of educators. Each team member at an interview should have the questions ahead of time with a rating scale and comment area. Interviewers should keep an open mind and discuss each potential candidate as a group. One interviewer may see or recognize a trait that another might miss. The interview process also lets you gain an insight on how the applicant reacts under pressure, how he uses body language, and how well he can communicate ideas and philosophies.

The team should use questions that are knowledge-based and about classroom management, mixing those with some questions about a candidate's experiences. DO NOT ask about his/her private life. Concentrate questions on the position for which the applicant is interviewing. Ask the same questions to all the candidates. Narrow the field and reach a consensus. If that is not possible, you may wish to call back the applicants who look most promising and interview them a second time. Always thank the applicant for coming in.

Questions Need to Be Varied

- **Ask questions focused on instructional skills and knowledge;**

- **Ask about classroom management style;**

- **Ask about communications skills with parents, students, and colleagues;**

- **Ask about past educational experiences in classroom settings, either as a teacher or an intern;**

- **Ask how they would handle certain scenarios (misbehaviors, irate parents, workload, paperwork); and**

- **Ask questions about training for this job and how to handle certain situations.**

The Interview Process

The Interview Itself

- Introduce everyone in the room.
- Start with small talk just to get the applicant comfortable. Begin with easy questions, such as asking him to describe his educational experiences or talk about where he went to school.
- Maintain eye contact and stay focused.
- Ask questions in a simple format.
- Explain why everyone is writing while he is speaking, to help put the candidate at ease.
- Stick to the interview plan and time constraints.
- Allow the applicant to answer the question, but do not let him get off topic.
- Never show a reaction to any of the answers presented.
- Offer a tour of the building so he can catch the flavor of the school.
- Thank the applicant for coming in.

Topics to Avoid in an Interview

- Age
- Race
- Religion
- Number of children
- Pregnancy plans
- Political beliefs
- Retirement plans
- Sexual orientation
- Marital status
- Health status
- Opinions on unions

Communicating With the Media

- Know what you are talking about.
- Be careful with careless responses; think first, speak second.
- Don't fear silences and pauses; use the time to frame your answers.
- Answer the question; don't give a speech.
- Keep answers short; don't let your point get lost in a maze of words.
- Stay away from jargon; it's a foreign language.
- Don't say anything you don't want to see in print.
- Don't talk "off the record"; nothing is off the record.
- Never say "No Comment"; it sounds suspicious.
- If you don't know, say so, and offer to find out.
- If you know, but can't say, explain why.
- Turn negative questions into positive answers.
- Ignore hypothetical questions; stick to the facts, not fiction.
- Use your own words; don't let the reporter put his words in your mouth.
- Express your own opinions; don't echo the reporter's.
- Don't lie; if you can't tell the truth, don't speak.
- Be accurate; if you are not sure, say so.
- Get your facts straight; give consistent responses.
- Be confident; you may not know it all, but you know more than the reporter.
- Don't ask to review the story before it is printed; it's not going to happen.
- Don't pick fights with people in the media; they never run out of ink or airtime.
- Don't use words to agitate a controversy; calmly explain your position.
- Share the praise; turn "me" upside down to "we" for positive stories.
- Don't be condescending, sarcastic, or flippant; quotes can turn on you.
- Stay aware that what you say may be quoted, so be careful how you say it.
- Brush off criticisms and misquotes; readers and listeners have short memories.
- Take time to say "Thank You" for the good and accurate stories.

Guidelines to Writing a Good Press Release

Whenever you have an extraordinary event or a student or staff member who has won an award or achieved a special goal, let your community know about it by writing a press release. Ask your staff and parent organization leaders to assist you, using the following guidelines:

- **Write about how unique the experience was.**
- **Highlight the aspects that make it newsworthy.**
- **Make it upbeat and positive.**
- **Target the newspaper or local media in your school's community.**
- **Report on activities that included parents and community leaders, not just the students.**
- **Make sure the facts, dates, and times are correct.**
- **Make sure spelling is correct.**
- **Check the registration forms to see if the parents allow their child's name and photograph to be used by the media.**
- **Limit the story or press release to no more than one page.**
- **Write it in such a way that not just the parents and students of your school would want to read this, but outsiders as well. Remember the big picture.**
- **If it is a seasonal event, give the media enough time. They may want to come out and do the story and pictures themselves.**

Appendix B
Bringing the Art of Communication to You

Dear Professional Development Coordinator:

Thank you for considering one of our breakthrough programs for your next event. We look forward to having the opportunity to offer your staff a motivational, thought-provoking, fun program, rich in both content and humor. Our list of clients includes teachers, principals, superintendents, and others who want to become effective communicators.

Here's what we want you to know more than anything else . . .

We understand firsthand the freedom that comes with communicating effectively. Like you, we have been there in the trenches, and from our experiences, we have created a continuum of effective techniques thousands of individuals have used to achieve successful communication. But good communication is an ongoing exercise, and for people to continue to learn and to use the tools we offer, those tools must be easy to access. To that end, we have written the book *Principal Talk!* which we can also have available to complement our program.

Learning how to effectively communicate is a necessity for the professional educator. People who know how to communicate well can head off problems before they arise, build strong relationships, create partnerships, and chart a path for students, parents, and teachers to travel together.

Which is a better expenditure of time, money, and effort: constantly having to remedy the problems that result from communication breakdowns, or being able to address difficult situations proactively through skilled communication? The choice is clear: knowing how to communicate effectively is essential, and we can teach your staff that skill.

Our programs have been tried and tested to provide you with first-class, professional information and materials. You can choose from a wide variety of our proven courses or have us customize one for your staff's needs.

Contact us and tell us your communication challenge. We want to help you make your next professional development event a communication success!

Regards,
Cheli Cerra, M.Ed.
Ruth Jacoby, Ed.D.

P.S. When you want your people to communicate effectively, so that misunderstandings no longer steal time and create hard feelings, contact Cheli and Ruth for a customized, personalized, hands-on, humor-based keynote or seminar.
Check our website at **http://www.school-talk.com.** The quicker you respond, the faster your staff will begin to learn how to communicate effectively.

www.school-talk.com

Our Programs Are First-Class

www.school-talk.com

Let's Talk!: Learning the Art of Effective Communication.

A successful communicator knows his audience and how to get his point across without creating any misunderstandings. In this hands-on, fun, and informative program, your staff will learn the tools necessary to begin artfully communicating with others. They will learn how to:

- **Use key words to defuse hostile situations;**
- **Listen effectively;**
- **Clearly convey their point to get their message heard; and**
- **Create positive relationships through effective communication.**

Cheli and Ruth use hands-on, personal experiences and real-life case studies to demonstrate and teach the tools necessary in learning the art of effective communication.

Book this program for your next meeting or convention and let Cheli and Ruth teach the staff within your organization the steps necessary to diffuse hostile situations, learn the art of listening, and create a positive communication-friendly environment.

In this eye-opening workshop, the presenters will provide
the participants with a self-assessment skills test that will
reveal their personal communication comfort level. From
this self-assessment, the audience will begin to map their
own personal blueprint for communication success.

Cheli and Ruth use situations, snapshots, and activities to
involve the audience. This interactive workshop is fun and
informative. Participants will learn how to:

- **Use key phrases to capture attention;**
- **Talk effortlessly through difficult communication
  situations; and**
- **Learn the number one secret to effective
  communication.**

Book this program for your staff today and have them
leave with a personal communication blueprint that they
can begin to implement immediately.

About the Authors

About Cheli Cerra

For more than 18 years, she has helped thousands of children achieve school and life success. As a school principal, and a mother of two, Cheli knows firsthand the issues that teachers, parents and children face. She was the founding principal of one of the first K-8 schools in Miami-Dade County, Florida, Everglades Elementary. The school of 1,500 students received an "A+" rating from the Florida Department of Education for two consecutive years under Cheli's leadership.

Cheli is the founder of **Eduville.com**, a life-long learning community. Her company provides resources and strategies for parents and teachers to help their children achieve school and life success, as well as continue the love of life-long learning. Among her resources are Smarter Kid Secrets, a free monthly e-zine, and her website **http://www.eduville.com,** full of tips, techniques, and strategies useful for anyone interested in helping a child succeed.

Recognized as **"The Right Choice"** by *Woman's Day Magazine,* and featured on over 30 radio shows throughout the country, Cheli is committed to education. Because of her leadership expertise, Cheli was invited to join twelve other experts in authoring *Real World Leadership Strategies That Work,* published by Insight Publishing.

Cheli is committed to helping teachers and parents come together for the success of children. Her seminars, coaching programs, and presentations have provided strategies that empower her audiences to action. She will captivate you by teaching the lessons learned from her in-the-trenches experience in public education. As a wife and working mother of two, she understands the reality of everyday life and creates strategies to meet these challenges quickly and easily. Her powerful message of immigrating to this country, learning the language, and adapting to a new culture, also give Cheli a unique insight to the real-world challenges children face today.

About Dr. Ruth Jacoby

Dr. Ruth is the founding principal of the Somerset Academy charter schools, which include five charter schools with 1,250 students in pre-kindergarten through tenth grade. She has more than 30 years of experience as an administrator and educator, in traditional public, private, and charter schools. Under her leadership, Somerset Charter School became one of the first charter schools to receive SACS (Southern Association of Colleges and Schools) accreditation. Her middle school received an "A+" rating from the Florida Department of Education in its first year of operation.

Dr. Ruth received her Ed.D. degree in Child and Youth Studies for Children from Birth through 18 Years from Nova Southeastern University, and her Masters of Science in Special Needs and Bachelor of Science in Early Childhood and Elementary Education from Brooklyn College.

During the past three years, Dr. Ruth has become actively involved in educating other charter school personnel in how to develop standards-based curriculum and assessments. Her school was one of the founding partners of the Tri-County Charter School Partnership, which has implemented three South Florida Annenberg Challenge grants in student assessment and school accountability and two Florida Charter School Dissemination Grants. She serves on several governing boards for charter schools in Miami-Dade and Broward County, Florida, and is an active member of the Florida Consortium of Charter Schools.

A Very Special Thanks to:
Our husbands: Tom Cerra and Marty Jacoby, for their unconditional love;
Our children: Alexandra, Frank, Sari, and Scott, for their patience;
Our editors: Vicki McCown and Paula Wallace, for their thoroughness;
Our designer: Henry Corona, for his continuous creativity;
All of the teachers, students, parents, and community leaders
who have touched our lives;
Our wonderful staff; colleagues; and outstanding
schools; and you, our reader, for reading,
absorbing, learning, sharing,
and growing.

"Effective communicators always leave a piece of wisdom with their audience."

To your artful and effective communication.

Cheli and Ruth

Let us hear from you . . . send us your snapshots. Email Cheli and Ruth at:

Cheli Cerra
Cheli@school-talk.com

Ruth Jacoby
DrRuth@school-talk.com

The *School Talk!* Series
by Cheli Cerra, M.Ed. and Ruth Jacoby, Ed.D.

Parent Talk! The Art of Effective Communication With the School and Your Child

This must-have guide for parents provides 52 "snapshots" of just about every conceivable situation than can arise between a parent, a student, and a school and provides clear, simple suggestions for positive solutions. From "My child's friend is a bad influence" to "I don't understand the results from my child's test," it covers all the typical events in a student's school experience.

ISBN 0-471-72013-5   **Paperback**   **www.josseybass.com**

Teacher Talk! The Art of Effective Communication

"An amazing compilation of what to say to parents. This book is a must have for your professional library."

—*Harry K. Wong, Ed.D., author of the bestselling* The First Days of School

An essential guidebook for all teachers that presents effective strategies for handling 52 common situations and simple ways to communicate with students, parents, and administrators. Features worksheets, checklists, sample letters, and more.

ISBN 0-471-72014-3   **Paperback**   **www.josseybass.com**

Principal Talk! The Art of Effective Communication in Successful School Leadership

"*Principal Talk!* provides simple communication strategies and advice to keep teachers, students, parents, staff, and the community in your corner. A must-read for today's educational leader to be successful in today's reform climate."

—*Jack Canfield, co-author,* Chicken Soup for the Teacher's Soul

This user-friendly, quick reference presents 52 "snapshots" of communication issues faced by busy principals and assistant principals in working with staff, parents, teachers, and the community.

ISBN 0-7879-7911-2   **Paperback**   **www.josseybass.com**

School Board Talk! The Art of Effective Communication

For both the aspiring and the veteran school board members, this book offers tips, worksheets, and practical advice to help board members develop and improve communication skills, survive in political office, and make a difference in education. In its user-friendly, easy-to-browse pages you'll find 50 "snapshots" and solution strategies on topics such as: casting the lone "no" vote and surviving, keeping your family in your fan club, building a school board team, handling constituent calls, and conquering the e-mail and memo mountain.

ISBN 0-7879-7912-0   **Paperback**   **www.josseybass.com**